NICK'S SKI RESORT GUIDEBOOK

WHISTLER BLACKCOMB

NICHOLAS WILLIAM JONES

Paperback ISBN: 978-1-990717-16-1
Ebook ISBN: 978-1-990717-17-8

Editing and production by The Self-Publishing Studio: www.self-publishingstudio.com

ACKNOWLEDGEMENTS

I would like to express my gratitude to all my friends, fellow skiers, photographers, partners, and sponsors who played a significant role in making this guidebook a reality. Without their support, guidance, and expertise, writing this book would not have been possible.

A big thanks goes out to FATMAP.com for allowing me to use screen captures from their FATMAP app. This has allowed me to easily include many different views to illustrate what I describe in the guidebook. I would also like to thank Whistler Blackcomb/Vail for letting me use screen captures from their Winter Trail Map.

Special thanks also goes out to those who introduced me to Whistler Blackcomb, the resort that I have had the privilege to ski at for 15+ years. Their passion for skiing and love for this resort helped me to discover its unique features and hidden gems and inspired me to share this knowledge with other skiers through this guidebook.

I am deeply grateful to those who have reviewed this guidebook and provided suggestions for improvement. Your insights have been invaluable in shaping this guide. I would also like to thank everyone who generously shared their photos of skiing at Whistler Blackcomb and who gave me permission to use those photos in this guidebook.

And finally, thanks to my wonderful son Owen Jones Cree and daughter Alex Jones Cree—amazing big-mountain skiers in their own right—for their love and support for my work on this guidebook.

Nick Jones
West Vancouver, BC, Canada
nick@jones.ca
778-996-0568

Legal Disclaimer

By using this guidebook, the reader agrees to release the author from any and all liability, claims, or causes of action arising from using this book or skiing activities at the Whistler Blackcomb Resort.

This guidebook is intended to provide general information about skiing at the Whistler Blackcomb Resort. While due care was taken in preparing this book, the author makes no guarantees as to the accuracy or completeness of the information provided. **The author accepts no responsibility for any errors or omissions and expressly disclaims any liability for any damages or injuries that may result from the use of this book.**

Skiing can be a dangerous activity, and users of this guidebook assume all risks associated with skiing at Whistler Blackcomb. **It is the responsibility of the user of this guidebook to ensure that they ski safely within the boundaries and according to the rules of the Whistler Blackcomb Resort as outlined on this website:**

https://www.whistlerBlackcomb.com/the-mountain/more-options/safety.aspx

If you are at all unsure about your skiing skills or skiing at the Whistler Blackcomb Resort, the author strongly recommends that you take a lesson or receive instruction from a qualified Whistler Blackcomb Resort ski instructor before skiing on Whistler Blackcomb. You can find information about lessons at Whistler Blackcomb here:

https://www.whistlerblackcomb.com

TABLE OF CONTENTS

INTRODUCTION

About the Author

I have lived in British Columbia for the last 15+ years and have spent an equal number of seasons skiing at Whistler Blackcomb. I love to spend time outside on the slopes skiing with friends, family, and visitors and exploring both mountains. My dream is to create ski resort guides for all the major ski resorts in Alberta and British Columbia (and perhaps beyond).

- www.jones.ca
- https://www.instagram.com/bcnnick/

About this Guidebook

Nick's Ski Resort Guide, Whistler Blackcomb provides an overview of Whistler Blackcomb's skiing terrain, including the different areas on the two mountains, trail maps, and descriptions of runs and other features and facilities. This guidebook also includes tips and recommendations for different skill levels so you can find the best runs for your abilities. Additionally, it provides information on skiing safety, insider tips on when to ski to avoid crowds, and recommendations on where to ski in different weather conditions.

My hope is that this guidebook will help you gain insight into Whistler Blackcomb as if you were talking to a local who has skied the mountains for many years.

Who is this guidebook for?

This guidebook is primarily designed for visitors who are planning to ski at Whistler Blackcomb for the first time and want to learn about the different areas, specific runs, and the various gondolas, lifts, and facilities on the two mountains. This guidebook may also be of interest to occasional visitors who want to become more familiar with the resort.

Homeowners in the Whistler Blackcomb area who rent out their place to visitors might also find this guidebook to be a great addition so that their guests can use it to learn about skiing at the resort. Hotels (or other accommodation), ski stores, and other stores in the Whistler Blackcomb area might also consider this guidebook to offer for sale to customers in their stores.

How to use this guidebook?

To make the most of your skiing experience at Whistler Blackcomb, I recommend that you read through the guidebook before you arrive at the mountain (or in the mornings and evenings while you are at the resort). This will help you familiarize yourself with the different areas, the terrain, the lifts, and other essential information that will help you make the most of your time at the resort.

While you're skiing, I recommend using the **FATMAP mobile app** on your cell phone. FATMAP provides great 3D views of the mountains enhanced by overlays of trails and other information. I have been working with the FATMAP team to improve the presentation of the runs on Whistler Blackcomb in their mobile app. This is an ongoing process, and I would welcome any suggestions for improvement that anyone might want to share.

- **Android:** https://play.google.com/store/apps/details?id=com. fatmaprn
- **Apple:** https://apps.apple.com/us/app/fatmap-ski-hike-bike/ id1294681561

Another mobile app to consider is the **Epic Mix app** from Whistler Blackcomb/Vail. The Epic Mix app provides a digital copy of the resort trail map, real-time information about lift statuses, approximate queue times, ski conditions, and the locations of restaurants and other amenities.

- https://www.epicpass.com/benefits/epicmix

Finally, **Openskimap.org** is a great online resource for trail information and is regularly updated by contributors.

- https://openskimap.org/

FATMAP

The best app for the outdoors

3D maps for hikers, bikers, skiers and mountaineers

Skiers and snowboarders coming up the Harmony Express Chairlift with 7th Heaven in the background (Source: Nick Jones).

SKIING SAFETY

Whistler Blackcomb is a large resort with a wide variety of runs and terrain that range in difficulty and include a range of big-mountain hazards. Whistler Blackcomb also experiences a wide range of weather and snow conditions. As a result, ski safety while skiing at the resort is an important consideration and worthy of attention.

Trail Difficulty

The difficulty of runs at Whistler Blackcomb are color coded as follows:

●	Green runs:	Easy runs, typically wide with a slope gradient of less than 25%.
■	Blue runs:	Intermediate runs generally have a slope between 25–40%.
◆	Black runs:	Expert runs, steep gradients exceeding 40% and difficult terrain.
◆◆	Double-Black runs:	Expert only, most difficult runs. Gradients greater than 40%, very difficult features and terrain.

Some runs in this guidebook are identified as Triple Black. This is based on feedback I have received from expert skiers and references on other trail maps. Triple-Black runs (sometimes also called Proline runs) are at the very extreme edge of difficulty and should only be considered by highly experienced, expert, freeride skiers.

Whistler Blackcomb Size and Difficulty

Compared to other hills, everything at Whistler Blackcomb is a scale bigger. I have heard visitors say "Wow...that Blue was like a Black on the hill where I usually ski!" Just because this guidebook or the Whistler Blackcomb Trail Map says Green or Blue or Black, don't necessarily associate that with the difficulty you're used to on your home hill. Always approach new runs at the resort with caution and get a feel for them before committing.

Range of Blues and Greens

Please also note that there is a wide range of each type of run in the Whistler Blackcomb Resort area. In particular, some Blue runs are actually very dark Blue verging on Black in steepness and difficulty. I have even suggested to the resort that they should really have a Double-Blue designation for the more difficult Blue runs. The same goes for some Greens that are more like Lite Blue in terms of difficulty—maybe Double Greens?

The difficulty of a run also greatly varies depending on whether it has been groomed recently or not (is it smooth or bumpy?) and whether there is fresh/good snow or if it is icy/bare. A run that is a challenging Blue on a good day may be more like a Black run on a day with poor visibility or poor snow conditions.

If you are new to Whistler Blackcomb, always visually check a run before skiing down it. If there are other skiers, ask if they have skied the run already and if they have any feedback on it. Know your limits and ski safely within the range of your ability.

If you are looking for easy routes to get through an area or to get down the mountain, look for the signs that indicate these routes. These signs are placed at major intersections and all along the easy routes.

Hazards

The Whistler Blackcomb Resort includes a huge skiing area (8,171 acres or 33.07 square kilometers) with a wide range of terrain and features. Many of these are big-mountain hazards that are not normally encountered at smaller ski resorts and need to be kept in mind when skiing at Whistler.

Avalanches

Avalanches are caused by a combination of factors, such as snowpack conditions, terrain, weather, and human triggers. Snowpack stability plays a crucial role, with weak layers beneath denser layers being prone to collapse under pressure. Steep slopes, especially those between 30° and 45°, are particularly prone to avalanches. Weather conditions like heavy snowfall, rapid temperature changes, and strong winds can contribute to snowpack instability. Human activities, like skiing and snowboarding, can also trigger avalanches by adding stress to the snowpack.

To avoid avalanches, educate yourself on avalanche safety, assessing snowpack conditions, and recognizing potential hazards. Regularly check local avalanche forecasts to understand the risk level in the area. Choose terrain and routes wisely, considering slope angle, aspect, and terrain features. If you go into avalanche-prone areas, carry essential safety equipment, such as an avalanche beacon, shovel, and probe, and know how to use them. Travel with a partner and practice safe travel techniques, like skiing one at a time on avalanche-prone slopes. If you are going to be skiing in avalanche-prone areas, I highly recommend taking an avalanche safety course if you plan to venture into the backcountry or alpine environments.

- **Avalanche basics information:** https://www.rei.com/learn/expert-advice/avalanche-basics.html
- **Avalanche safety training:** https://themountainschool.com/product-category/avalanche/

Cornices

A cornice is a large overhanging mass of snow and ice that forms along the edge of a ridge, cliff, or other elevated terrain feature. Cornices are created by the accumulation of windblown snow that adheres to the leeward (downwind) side of the ridge or slope. Over time, the snow compacts and forms a projecting ledge that can extend horizontally outward from the terrain.

Cornices can pose a significant hazard to skiers, snowboarders, and mountaineers. They may be unstable and can break off suddenly, causing an avalanche or a fall. It can also be difficult to determine the exact edge of a cornice, as the overhang might be obscured by snow. To minimize the risk associated with cornices, it is important to maintain a safe distance from the edge of a bowl or cliff, approach edges with caution, and avoid traversing directly beneath cornices.

- **Cornice hazards overview:** https://www.mountainskillsacademy.com/cornice-hazards-need-know/

Cornices hanging over Harmony Horseshoe Bowl chutes.
(Source: Nick Jones)

Steep and Difficult Terrain

Steep terrain can pose a significant danger to skiers, as the increased slope angle heightens the risk of falls, avalanches, and losing control. On steep slopes, even a minor mistake or loss of balance can result in a high-speed fall, potentially leading to serious injuries or collisions with obstacles such as rocks, trees, or other skiers. Additionally, steep slopes are more prone to avalanches, with slopes between 30° and 45° being particularly hazardous. In the event of an avalanche, the steepness of the slope can significantly contribute to the speed and force of the snow, increasing the risk of injury—or even fatality—for those caught in the slide.

To avoid the hazards associated with steep terrain, you should take precautions including:

- Ensure that you have the appropriate skill level and experience to tackle steep slopes safely. Gradually progressing to steeper terrain as your skills and confidence improve can help prevent accidents caused by skiing beyond your ability.

- Choose routes wisely, considering slope angle, snow conditions, and potential avalanche risk. You should familiarize yourself with the terrain by studying maps, consulting guidebooks, or seeking local knowledge.
- Skiing with a buddy or a group provides additional safety, as partners can help each other identify hazards and assist in case of an emergency.
- Ensure that you have the proper equipment such as helmets, avalanche beacons, a shovel, and a probe.
- Maintain a strong awareness of your surroundings, including other skiers and potential hazards, to help reduce the risks associated with skiing on steep terrain.

Tree Wells

Tree wells are hidden hazards that skiers and snowboarders may encounter, particularly in areas with heavy snowfall and dense tree coverage. They form when snow accumulates around the base of a tree, creating a cone-shaped depression underneath the branches. The tree's branches and foliage prevent snow from packing tightly around the trunk, leaving the area around the tree loosely packed or hollow. This concealed depression can pose a significant danger to skiers and snowboarders. Falling into a tree well may result in injuries from the fall, entrapment, or even suffocation if the individual becomes buried and unable to move.

To avoid the hazards posed by tree wells, you can take several precautions:

- Always ski or snowboard with a buddy when venturing into areas where tree wells are likely to be found. This ensures that someone is available to help or call for assistance if one person becomes trapped. Additionally, maintaining visual contact and establishing a communication plan with your partner can help ensure a quick response in case of emergency.
- When skiing or snowboarding near trees, be aware of the potential presence of tree wells and maintain a safe distance from tree trunks. Maintain proper technique and control while skiing or snowboarding to prevent falls and minimize the likelihood of ending up in a tree well.

Mondays Issac Brengelmann on the wall beside Mondays above West Bowl on Whistler.
A great example of steep and challenging terrain. (Source: Dave Brengelmann)

- In case of a fall near a tree, try to avoid going headfirst and use your arms to create an airspace around your face to prevent suffocation. Carrying a whistle or other signaling device can help alert your partner if you become trapped.
- Familiarize yourself with basic tree well rescue techniques and regularly practice them with your partner in order to improve your ability to respond effectively in case of an emergency.

Tree well dangers overview: https://www.helicat.org/safety-risk-awareness/2021/2/11/tree-well-dangers

On-Hill Signage

Whistler Blackcomb employs a variety of signs on the two mountains to inform skiers of risks, run conditions, and other important safety issues. Watch out for signs and obey them. Examples of signs include:

- **CLOSED:** These signs mark off areas that are closed for use. If you cross into a closed area, you risk losing your pass if you are caught by the ski patrol.
- **Ski Area Boundary:** These signs mark the edge of the Whistler Blackcomb ski area. Anything beyond these signs is unpatrolled and may include significant risk if entered.
- **SLOW Zone:** These are large yellow banners stretched across some runs to indicate that the area is a slow-skiing area for beginners. Please respect the slow zones for your safety and that of the other skiers.

For more information about Whistler Blackcomb signage, visit:

https://www.whistlerblackcomb.com/the-mountain/more-options/safety.aspx

KNOW AND RESPECT THESE COMMON SIGNS ON THE MOUNTAIN

CLOSED means CLOSED.

Indicates an area is permanently closed for safety reasons including cliff or cornice danger.

Indicates a run/area is closed for safety reasons due to active avalanche bombing or high avalanche danger.

The area beyond this boundary is hazardous backcountry terrain. Persons proceeding beyond this point should be prepared for avalanche danger, weather changes, terrain hazards and be equipped and trained for self-rescue.

Indicates Uphill Travel within the Whistler Blackcomb ski area boundary is only permitted on designated routes, marked with signage.

Source: https://www.whistlerblackcomb.com/the-mountain/more-options/safety.aspx

Alpine Responsibility Code

Whistler Blackcomb has a clear code of conduct that skiers and snowboarders on the two mountains are expected to follow. The Whistler Blackcomb Mountain Safety Team, Ski Patrol, and Terrain Park Rangers will stop and let you know when you are not following the code. Failure to follow the Alpine Responsibility Code could result in a range of consequences, including losing your pass. At the most extreme, you could face a lifetime suspension from Whistler Blackcomb.

Snow Conditions

Snow conditions at Whistler Blackcomb can change dramatically hour to hour and day to day, significantly impacting skiing conditions. Weather patterns, sunlight, temperature fluctuations, and wind can all contribute to these rapid shifts. Fresh snowfall overnight can create a delightful layer of powder for eager skiers in the morning, only for the snow to transform into heavy, wet, and challenging conditions by the afternoon due to rising temperatures. It is crucial for skiers and snowboarders to be aware of changing snow conditions so that they can adapt their plans and ensure that they have the best possible experience on the slopes.

- **Different types of snow:** https://www.exceptionalstays.com/explore/ski-weather-perfection-different-types-of-snow-conditions/

Weather

Whistler Blackcomb is known for its varied and changing weather conditions. On any given day, skiers and snowboarders can experience a wide variety of weather, ranging from clear, sunny days with bluebird skies to heavy snowfall, fog, and even rain at lower elevations. Temperatures at Whistler Blackcomb can vary significantly, with the base area generally experiencing milder conditions and the alpine regions being considerably colder. In the winter months, temperatures can range from 5°C to 10°C and can drop as low as -25°C or lower at higher elevations. Wind speeds can also be unpredictable, with gusts reaching up to 120 kilometers per hour or more during intense storm systems, resulting in reduced visibility and wind-chill effects.

ALPINE RESPONSIBILITY CODE

THERE ARE ELEMENTS OF RISK THAT COMMON SENSE AND PERSONAL AWARENESS CAN HELP REDUCE. REGARDLESS OF HOW YOU DECIDE TO USE THE SLOPES, ALWAYS SHOW COURTESY TO OTHERS. PLEASE ADHERE TO THE CODE LISTED BELOW AND SHARE WITH OTHERS THE RESPONSIBILITY FOR A SAFE OUTDOOR EXPERIENCE.

1 *Always stay in control. You must be able to stop, or avoid other people or objects.*

2 *People ahead of you have the right-of-way. It is your responsibility to avoid them.*

3 *Do not stop where you obstruct a trail or are not visible from above.*

4 *Before starting downhill or merging onto a trail, look uphill and yield to others.*

5 *If you are involved in or witness a collision or accident, you must remain at the scene and identify yourself to the Ski Patrol.*

6 *Always use proper devices to help prevent runaway equipment.*

7 *Observe and obey all posted signs and warnings.*

8 *Keep off closed trails and closed areas.*

9 *You must not use lifts or terrain if your ability is impaired through use of alcohol or drugs.*

10 *You must have sufficient physical dexterity, ability and knowledge to safely load, ride and unload lifts. If in doubt, ask the lift attendant.*

Know the Code - Be Safety Conscious
It is Your Responsibility

CANADA WEST SKI AREAS ASSOCIATION

Proudly Supported By
KAL TIRE

10/2010
© CWSAA

Source: https://www.whistlerblackcomb.com/the-mountain/more-options/safety.aspx

The weather experienced at Whistler Blackcomb during the winter season is influenced by several factors. The resort's location in the Pacific Northwest exposes the area to moist, maritime air masses originating from the Pacific Ocean. These air masses often bring significant precipitation, which falls as snow in the colder months, contributing to the resort's abundant snowfall. The topography of the Coast Mountains also plays a crucial role in shaping the local weather patterns. As moist air is forced to rise over the mountainous terrain, it cools and condenses, resulting in the formation of clouds and precipitation as rain or in winter as snow.

Temperature inversions are another notable weather phenomenon at Whistler Blackcomb, caused by cold air getting trapped in the valley while warmer air remains at higher elevations. This can lead to cooler temperatures in the base areas, with more pleasant conditions in the alpine regions. Lastly, the resort's latitude and proximity to Arctic air masses can result in colder temperatures and more extreme weather systems during the winter months. These factors combine to create the dynamic and ever-changing weather conditions experienced at Whistler Blackcomb, making it essential for skiers and snowboarders to be prepared for a wide range of conditions.

Check both the Whistler Blackcomb official websites and other weather websites to determine the weather forecast for a day on Whistler Blackcomb:

- **Whistler Blackcomb weather forecast:** https://www.whistlerblackcomb.com/the-mountain/mountain-conditions/snow-and-weather-report.aspx
- **Mountain-forecast.com:** https://www.mountain-forecast.com/peaks/Whistler-Mountain-BC/forecasts/2181

Avalanche Control

Avalanche control is an essential safety measure undertaken by the Whistler Blackcomb Ski Patrol to protect both guests and employees. This activity is focused on reducing the risk of avalanches by intentionally triggering smaller, controlled slides to remove unstable layers of snow. The ski patrol team works diligently to assess and monitor snowpack stability, utilizing a variety of tools such as explosives, ski cutting, and cornice drops. They also analyze weather data, snowpack history, and recent avalanche activity to make informed decisions about potential hazards. Regular avalanche control efforts allow ski resorts to maintain safe terrain and reduce the risk of large, destructive avalanches, ensuring a safer and more enjoyable experience for everyone on the mountain.

Avalanches coming down from the ridge and cornices above the Saudan Couloir. (Source: Nick Jones)

Unexploded avalanche control bombs pose a rare but serious hazard to skiers and snowboarders venturing off-piste (away from controlled terrain). These devices may have failed to detonate during avalanche control operations and can remain hidden under the snow. To avoid encountering unexploded ordnance, it is crucial to adhere to resort boundaries, obey all posted signage, and respect any closures or warnings. If you happen to come across an object resembling an unexploded rocket or bomb while skiing or snowboarding, it is critical to maintain a safe distance and avoid touching or disturbing it. Immediately report the location and description of the suspicious item to the Whistler Blackcomb Ski Patrol to ensure proper handling and disposal by trained professionals.

- **Avalanche control:** https://en.wikipedia.org/wiki/Avalanche_control

Emergency Assistance

In the event of a medical emergency or skiing accident on the slopes of Whistler Blackcomb, the ski patrol team is ready to assist. If you need help, call the **Whistler Blackcomb Ski Patrol dispatch at +1 604-935-5555**. Alternatively, you can ask a nearby ski instructor or resort staff member to use their radio to call for assistance. Make sure to provide clear information about your location, the nature of the incident, and any injuries sustained to ensure a rapid and appropriate response. The Whistler Blackcomb Ski Patrol is equipped to handle a wide range of situations, from minor injuries to serious accidents, and has a variety of methods to bring injured skiers down from the mountain. Most of the ski patrol's Skidoos are equipped with beepers to alert skiers as they go up or down runs.

- **Whistler Blackcomb mountain safety:** https://www. whistlerblackcomb.com/the-mountain/more-options/safety.aspx

In Whistler Village, the Whistler Health Care Centre, located at 4380 Lorimer Road, is a well-equipped facility providing urgent care, X-ray, and laboratory services to address immediate medical needs. For more advanced care or emergencies, the nearest full-service hospital is Squamish General Hospital, situated approximately 60 kilometers south of Whistler at 38140 Behrner Drive in Squamish. This hospital offers a 24-hour emergency room, inpatient care, diagnostic services, and a range of specialized medical services. Additionally, the surrounding area hosts numerous walk-in clinics, pharmacies, and private practices to cater to a variety of health-care needs.

WB Ski Patrol wrapping up Cliff Loh in a rescue sled before heading down the mountain.
(Source: Cliff Loh)

KIDS/YOUNGER SKIERS AND SNOWBOARDERS

Whistler Blackcomb has something for everyone, from beginners to world-class experts, so generally your kids will be able to have a good experience regardless of their ability level. Ideally, however, your kids should be comfortable with Blue runs. This will allow you to explore most of the resort with them and really appreciate what Whistler Blackcomb has to offer.

Preparation

When skiing/riding with young kids, it's very important to make sure they can stay warm, dry, and comfortable throughout the day. This also applies to adults, but as a parent, it is worth paying extra attention to kids' gear because they generally are more sensitive to conditions. You don't want foggy goggles or wet gloves to ruin the day for you and your kids. Hand and toe warmers are a good investment for cold days.

During the Day

When skiing with your kids, it is a good idea to pack some snacks so that you don't have to return to the lodge for food if your kids get hungry or low on energy. Returning to the lodge can take a lot of time in a big resort like Whistler Blackcomb. Chocolate, granola bars, or fruit bars that kids can eat in the lift line or on a chairlift are great energy sources. If possible, it is also good to have a flexible lunch time—either earlier or later—to avoid crowds that occur around midday at the lodges. Packing lunch to save yourself a visit to the lodge is also not a bad idea. This is especially helpful if you plan to visit areas like Symphony, where the hours of operation are quite limited, and you don't want to have to trek to the lodge in the middle of the day for lunch. Naturally, this also depends on your kids and whether they are comfortable with this (or they may need an in-lodge break in the middle of the day).

Max and Meredith Block having lunch on the mountain.
(Source: Jaye Block)

Contact Information

Remember to make sure that your kids know your phone number or have it on them. One option is to add a label or sticker with their name and your number to their helmet or clothing. This is especially important in a large resort like Whistler Blackcomb. Kids can sometimes accidentally get separated from their parents or their group. If this happens, they can always ask one of the resort staff or perhaps another skier or boarder to help them reconnect with their parents. This happens quite often, and the resort staff are great at helping kids with this.

On the Mountain

If possible, it is a good idea for kids to ski/ride with a buddy of similar ability level. This way, they can encourage each other, which helps make the day more enjoyable. For young kids, it's also easier if you have two adults—one can be in front leading the way while the other stays behind so he/she can watch the kids and help when needed.

It is also important that parents make sure their kids know what all the resort signs mean and respect them. The same goes for parents! Remember to be a role model for safe, respectful skiing.

Weather conditions can make a big difference for both parents and kids when on the mountain. Low visibility plus icy conditions can turn a mellow Blue run into a difficult Black run. This is especially true for kids. Keep an eye on conditions and make sure you are skiing in areas and conditions that will make the day enjoyable and safe for your kids.

A low visibility day on Whistler Blackcomb.
(Source: Jaye Block)

Powder Days

While we all like powder, powder snow can be very challenging for many kids. On a powder day, it can be quite frustrating for parents to deal with kids melting down because they keep falling or getting stuck instead of enjoying the conditions. If you know that your kids aren't comfortable with deep powder yet, consider leaving them in the hotel/lodge with one adult from your group. This way, other parents can fully enjoy fresh powder in the morning and pick up the kids around noon after most runs have been tracked out. Many kids don't ski/ride open-to-close anyway, so skiing for a full afternoon can be enough for them and result in the best possible experience for everyone.

Trees/Glades

Both Whistler and Blackcomb Mountain have many kid-friendly runs. The areas around the Emerald Express Chairlift have a lot of mellow, open Green/Blue runs that many kids like. This includes tree/glade runs specifically designed for kids. In these glade areas, there are runs in the middle that are not too difficult to navigate for kids who are comfortable with Blue runs. More experienced kids can then also venture into the trees off the main run. Kids who are comfortable with Black runs can go off-piste and stay in glades from near the top of the Emerald area all the way down to its base.

On Blackcomb, the middle part of the 7th Heaven Express Chairlift area has decent Blue glades that are kid friendly. If your kids are comfortable with Black runs, Arthur's Choice and Log Jam in the Crystal Express Chairlift area are good glade runs to consider.

It's a good idea to ask kids to always keep goggles on in the trees, as you never know when they are going to get too close to a branch. Ideally one adult should lead the way in the trees so that the group can stay clear of creeks and other dangers.

While most kids love the tight turns in trees and some may even want to do tree runs all day long, parents can help set the pace, so the kids don't get tired and be done with the day too early. Take snack breaks and try mixing up tree runs with groomers to add some variety and conserve energy.

Getting Back to Base

One final thought regarding kids: Plan the end of your day in advance. Depending on where you are on the mountain, it can take quite a bit of time to return to the base of the hill (or even to the top of a gondola). Keep an eye on your kids, and if they look like they are running out of steam, start heading back in the direction that will let you either download or ski out.

"Be safe is always the most important thing when skiing; after you do that, you can try to have fun; last, while having fun, try to improve and make sure you look good when skiing!" – Harper He (Source: Wenlei He)

SKIING GEAR

As you venture onto the slopes, the ski gear you choose will play a significant role in ensuring your comfort, performance, and safety. From helmets, skis, and goggles to clothing and accessories, each component contributes to a safe and enjoyable skiing experience.

Ski Boots

Ski boots are the critical connection between your body and your skis, playing a significant role in power transmission, control, and overall comfort. Many people say that good boots are the most important part of your gear. Poor-fitting boots can cause discomfort, pain, and reduced ski performance, ultimately detracting from your skiing experience. On the other hand, boots that fit well and are appropriately sized provide optimal support and stability, enabling skiers to maneuver effectively and maintain precise control over their movements.

A well-fitting boot should snugly wrap around the shape of your foot and lower leg, without causing excessive pressure points or leaving room for the foot to move around within the boot. Properly sized boots allow for enough space to wiggle your toes, while still providing a secure fit around the heel and ankle, minimizing the chances of blisters and discomfort. It is a good idea to try on several boot models and sizes and to consult with a ski store boot expert to find the best boots for your feet. A boot fitting, including heat molding and footbed adjustments, can further enhance the fit and comfort of your ski boots.

- **EVO – How to select ski boots:** https://www.evo.com/en-ca/guides/how-to-choose-and-size-ski-boots
- **REI – How to put on ski boots:** https://www.rei.com/learn/expert-advice/how-to-put-on-ski-boots-and-skis.html

Socks

Good-quality ski socks are also important because they wick moisture away from the skin, keeping your feet dry and reducing the risk of blisters. Sock materials like merino wool and synthetic blends offer excellent moisture-wicking properties as well as natural odor resistance and temperature regulation. A well-fitting sock should provide cushioning and support in key areas, such as the shin, heel, and the toe box, while avoiding bunching or wrinkling, which can cause pain points on your feet. Additionally, ski socks should fit snugly around the foot and calf, ensuring they stay in place throughout the day without sliding down or creating pressure points on your leg. Avoid wearing cotton socks, as they tend to absorb moisture and can lead to cold, damp feet.

- **REI – How to select ski socks:** https://www.rei.com/learn/expert-advice/how-to-choose-ski-and-snowboard-socks.html

Skis

Selecting skis that are the right size and type for your skill level and skiing style is important to ensure fun, safe, and good performance skiing. The right ski size and type can significantly impact your ability to control skiing, ensure stability, and allow you to improve your skiing skills. Beginners and intermediate skiers usually need shorter, more forgiving skis that enable easier turns and increased maneuverability. Advanced and expert skiers may opt for longer, stiffer skis designed for greater stability and control at high speeds.

Where you like to ski also plays a vital role in selecting the right ski type. All-mountain skis are great, general skis for various snow conditions and terrain types, making them a popular choice for recreational skiers at Whistler Blackcomb. Powder skis on the other hand, which are wider and have a rockered profile, really show their stuff by floating in deep, powder snow. Carving or race skis are perfect for ripping down hard, groomed runs, as the narrow waist and cambered profile allow for quick, precise turns.

Taking the time to research and ask ski shop experts for help can help you choose the best ski size and type for your needs. With the right skis, you can enhance your overall skiing experience, enabling you to safely ski, build confidence, and improve your skiing abilities.

- **EVO – How to choose a ski:** https://www.evo.com/en-ca/guides/how-to-choose-skis-size-chart
- **Stomp It – How to choose ski size:** https://www.youtube.com/watch?v=PKHIYjYaVBc

Ski and Snowboard Locks

Unfortunately, theft does happen on the mountains and in the village base areas (I had a pair of ski poles stolen from in front of the Glacier Creek Lodge on Blackcomb). Unattended, unlocked, high-value skis and ski poles are tempting targets for opportunistic thieves at the resort. I highly recommend investing in either a square lock (these fit into some ski racks on the mountain) or a wire lock (these work on all racks on the mountain) and that you lock up your gear when you are not using it. Locks are available in most shops on the mountain and in the village.

- **Sportchek – Ski lock:** https://www.sportchek.ca/product/ski-key-lock-258200005.html
- **Dakine – Cool lock (cable lock):** https://ce.dakine.com/products/cool-lock?variant=29226191749200

Helmet

A properly sized and adjusted helmet is a critical piece of your gear and significantly reduces the risk of head injuries, including concussions and skull fractures (my helmet has saved me more than once). A good ski helmet should fit snugly around the entire circumference of your head, without any uncomfortable pressure points or allowing excessive movement. When properly secured, the helmet should not shift or wobble as you move, ensuring consistent protection and coverage.

It is important to try on different helmet models and sizes, as head shapes and helmet designs can vary significantly. Look for a helmet that meets recognized safety standards and consider additional features such as adjustable vents for temperature regulation, removable ear pads for comfort, and compatibility with your ski goggles. Never compromise on fit or comfort, as a poor-fitting helmet can be less effective in providing adequate head protection.

- **REI – How to choose a helmet:** https://www.rei.com/learn/expert-advice/snow-helmet.html
- **Outdoor Gear Lab – How to choose a ski or snowboard helmet:** https://www.rei.com/learn/expert-advice/snow-helmet.html

Goggles

A good pair of ski goggles is another critical piece of ski gear designed to protect your eyes and optimize your vision on the slopes. High-quality goggles shield your eyes from harmful UV rays, wind, and blowing snow, helping to prevent eye strain, dryness, and potential damage. Well-fitting goggles should be comfortable but secure around your face, fit with your helmet, and maintain clear vision.

When selecting ski goggles, consider lens features such as UV protection, anti-fog coatings, and interchangeable lenses to accommodate varying light conditions. Goggles with a range of lens tints and VLT (Visible Light Transmission) percentages enable you to optimize your vision for different weather conditions, enhancing contrast and reducing glare. Additionally, consider frame size and shape to ensure compatibility with your facial structure and helmet, as well as venting systems to help maintain airflow and prevent fogging.

One key aspect of goggles is the color of the lens. Different lens colors are designed to work in different lighting conditions. On an overcast, cloudy day, a pink or rose-colored lens will help you see bumps and other features on runs that otherwise might be hard to see in the flat light. Similarly, on a bright, sunny day, a highly reflective blue, green, or red lens will tone down glare to improve your ability to see the run or other terrain features ahead of you.

- **Goggles'n'more – What color lens is best?** https://www.gogglesnmore.com/blog/what-color-lens-is-best-for-ski-goggles/
- **EVO – How to buy ski and snowboard goggles:** https://www.evo.com/en-ca/guides/how-to-buy-ski-snowboard-goggles-lens-size-fit

Face Protection

Wearing a face mask or balaclava while skiing in very cold conditions is important to protect your face and neck. A face covering will help prevent painful frostbite and will reduce the risk of hypothermia. Face coverings also shield the skin from harsh winds and harmful UV radiation, which can cause windburn and sunburn— even during the winter. Lastly, face coverings aid in moisture management by wicking away sweat, ensuring comfort and clear vision throughout the skiing experience.

Jacket and Pants

A good jacket and pants are important components of any ski or snowboarding outfit, as they will protect you from the elements and ensure optimal comfort while engaging in winter sports. The right jacket-and-pants combination will offer sufficient insulation, keeping you warm and cozy even in the coldest conditions. Breathable, moisture-wicking materials are also essential to regulate body temperature and prevent moisture build-up during periods of intense physical activity. Additionally, a well-designed jacket and pants will feature an adjustable fit, allowing for easy layering and freedom of movement without sacrificing protection from the elements.

Some key features to consider include:

- Waterproofing and seam sealing to protect you from snow, sleet, and rain, ensuring you stay dry and comfortable.
- Well-placed pockets and compartments allow for convenient storage of essential items such as ski passes, goggles, and snacks.
- Reinforced areas, like the knees and seat, that contribute to the longevity of your gear.
- Pit and leg zips that allow airflow into the jacket and pants on warm days.
- Arm and leg cuffs and a waist powder skirt to keep snow out of your jacket and pants.

Gloves

Maintaining hand comfort and dexterity is essential for both performance and safety in the unpredictable alpine conditions of

Whistler Blackcomb. Good ski gloves should be durable, waterproof, and breathable, with adequate insulation to retain warmth without sacrificing mobility. Well-fitted gloves ensure that you can grip your ski poles or adjust your gear effectively, minimizing the risk of cold-related injuries such as frostbite.

Inner Layers

Dressing in warm, moisture-wicking layers is an essential strategy for staying comfortable and safe during your skiing adventures at the resort. Layering effectively helps to regulate body temperature by trapping heat close to your skin, while also allowing for easy adjustments in response to changing weather conditions and activity levels.

Start with a moisture-wicking base layer made from synthetic or merino wool fabrics that effectively draw sweat away from your skin, preventing dampness and chills. Add a mid-layer, such as a fleece, for insulation and warmth. Follow that with a waterproof and breathable shell as outer layer to shield against wind, snow, and rain. This layering system will ensure that you maintain an optimal body temperature and stay dry throughout your skiing day.

Mobile Phone

Carrying a fully charged cell phone while skiing at Whistler Blackcomb is an important safety precaution, providing a lifeline in case of emergencies or unexpected situations. The ability to call for help or notify the ski patrol of any incidents is crucial, as it can significantly expedite response times and potentially prevent further complications or injuries. Additionally, cell phones allow for easy communication with fellow skiers and resort staff, ensuring you can stay connected and informed in rapidly changing conditions.

Mobile phones also provide access to mobile apps such as FATMAP to help find your way and plan where you want to ski next on the mountain. Another great app is the Epic Mix app from Vale/Whistler Blackcomb. This app provides trail maps, lift wait times, and other information to help manage your day.

It is important to store your device securely in a waterproof case to protect it from the elements and keep it close to your body to maintain battery life in cold temperatures.

Breakfast

Starting your day with a well-balanced, nutritious breakfast is crucial to fuel your body for a full day of skiing at Whistler Blackcomb. A hearty morning meal provides the necessary energy to support your physical exertion on the slopes while also enhancing your mental focus and endurance. Combine wholesome carbohydrates, lean proteins, and healthy fats to create a breakfast that will help keep you energized throughout the morning.

Snacks

Keeping your energy levels up is another important factor in ensuring a good day of skiing at Whistler Blackcomb. Pack easily portable and nutrient-dense snacks like trail mix, chocolate, energy bars, or fruit so that you can refuel between runs.

Lunch and Snacks

Maintaining proper nutrition during a day of skiing at Whistler Blackcomb is essential for sustaining energy levels, muscle recovery, and preventing fatigue. A well-rounded lunch will help you tackle the remainder of the ski day. Make or look for lunches that combine carbohydrates, lean proteins, and healthy fats, such as a sandwich with lean meats and plenty of veggies or a salad with protein. A balanced lunch will help to replenish your energy stores so that you can enjoy the rest of the ski day.

Après Ski

Whistler Blackcomb is renowned not only for its world-class skiing, but also for its vibrant après-ski scene, offering a wonderful opportunity to unwind, socialize, and celebrate after a day on the mountain. As you transition from the slopes to the bars and lounges, remember the importance of first rehydrating with water, as physical exertion and high altitudes during the day can lead to dehydration.

Prioritizing hydration helps to replenish lost fluids, support muscle recovery, and maintain overall well-being.

While enjoying the festive atmosphere, it's essential to keep alcohol consumption reserved for après-ski activities and refrain from drinking while on the hill. Consuming alcohol while skiing can impair judgment, coordination, and reaction time, increasing the risk of accidents or injuries.

Dinner

The Whistler Blackcomb Resort area boasts a diverse array of dining options, catering to a wide range of tastes and preferences. From casual eateries and cozy cafés to upscale restaurants and bars, the resort offers a range of choices.for all budgets and occasions. For those who prefer a more personalized dining experience or wish to unwind in the comfort of their accommodations, many lodgings in Whistler Blackcomb are equipped with full kitchens, allowing you to prepare your own meals with fresh, locally sourced ingredients from nearby stores and markets.

PASSES AND LIFT TICKETS

Whistler Blackcomb offers a variety of winter lift ticket options to suit every skier and snowboarder's needs. The resort offers a flexible ticketing system where guests can choose from single-day tickets for a quick ski getaway or multi-day passes for a more extended stay. Those seeking unlimited access to the slopes all winter long can purchase season passes that provide unrestricted skiing and riding throughout the season. Additionally, Whistler Blackcomb offers discounted lift tickets for children, seniors, and students, making it an ideal destination for families and students looking for a winter adventure.

The price of lift tickets at Whistler Blackcomb are certainly on the high end, but the quality, range, and area of skiing that you get at the resort is well worth it. Whistler Blackcomb is one of the largest ski resorts in North America and offers an amazing skiing experience for your money.

Whistler Blackcomb offers several lift ticket options for visitors to choose from.

Single-day and Multi-day Lift Tickets

These tickets grant access to the slopes for one day or more. They are perfect for anyone looking for a single day of skiing or perhaps multiple days in a row. Lift tickets can be purchased in person at the bottom of the hill or online in advance. Whistler Blackcomb also offers a refund under certain conditions.

- **Tickets:** https://www.whistlerblackcomb.com/plan-your-trip/lift-access/tickets.aspx
- **Refunds:** https://www.whistlerblackcomb.com/info/refund-request.aspx

Season Passes

There are a wide variety of season passes available. Three of the most popular ones are:

EDGE Cards

EDGE Cards are reloadable lift passes that offer flexibility and savings. Guests can choose between a one, three, five, or 10-day EDGE Card and enjoy discounted lift tickets for the selected number of days. EDGE Cards come with several benefits, including some access in the summer as well as discounts at local shops, restaurants, and hotels.

> **NOTE:** Edge Cards are only available to residents of Canada and Washington State.

WB Unlimited Season Pass

The Whistler Blackcomb Unlimited Season Pass provides unlimited access to the slopes throughout the winter season. They are ideal for frequent visitors or locals who want to enjoy the mountain all season long and are definitely worth it for those who plan to spend more than 15 days skiing at Whistler Blackcomb in one season. The pass comes with all sorts of benefits like summer lift access, tickets you can use with friends, discounts at other hills and at local shops, restaurants, and hotels.

Epic Pass

Whistler Blackcomb is part of the Epic Pass network, which offers access to multiple ski resorts worldwide. The Epic Pass provides access to Whistler Blackcomb along with other popular destinations, making it an excellent option for avid skiers and snowboarders who enjoy exploring different mountains. The Epic Pass offers the same benefits and resort discounts as the Unlimited Season Pass.

Always check online for the most recent updates regarding the costs of lift tickets and passes as well as the associated benefits and discounts.

- **Season passes:** https://www.whistlerblackcomb.com/plan-your-trip/lift-access/season-passes.aspx
- **Edge cards:** https://www.whistlerblackcomb.com/plan-your-trip/lift-access/edge-cards.aspx
- **WB Unlimited Season Pass:** https://www.whistlerblackcomb.com/plan-your-trip/lift-access/passes/unlimited-season-pass.aspx
- **Epic Pass:** https://www.epicpass.com/passes/epic-pass.aspx

WHISTLER BLACKCOMB RESORT

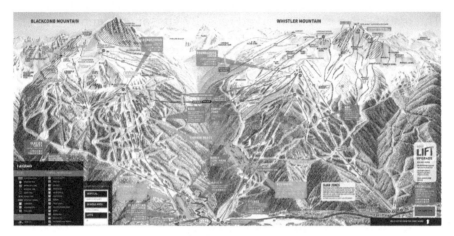

2022/23 Whistler Blackcomb Trail Map.
(Source: Whistler Blackcomb)

Whistler Blackcomb is a world-class ski resort located in the Coastal Mountains of British Columbia, Canada, about a two-hour drive north of Vancouver. It is one of the largest ski resorts in North America and attracts local visitors as well as guests from North America and around the world.

The Whistler area has a rich history that dates back thousands of years. The area was originally inhabited by the Squamish and Lil'wat First Nations, who hunted and fished in the region's mountains, forests, and rivers. In the 1800s, European settlers arrived and established the town of Alta Lake. Logging and mining were the main industries in the area until the 1960s, when a group of Vancouver businessmen discovered and started to develop the incredible skiing terrain in the surrounding mountains. They built the Whistler Mountain ski resort in the 1960s, and it quickly became a popular destination for winter sports enthusiasts.

As the name suggests, Whistler Blackcomb is comprised of two mountains—Whistler Mountain and Blackcomb Mountain. These mountains are joined by the Peak 2 Peak Gondola, one of the longest and highest gondolas in the world. Whistler Mountain opened for skiing in 1966 and Blackcomb opened in 1980. The two mountains merged in 1997 to create Whistler Blackcomb, one of the top ski resorts in the world.

Whistler Blackcomb encompasses a total of 8,171 acres or 33.07 square kilometers of skiable terrain, the largest in North America. The resort has over 200 marked runs, 37 lifts, and an impressive vertical drop of 5,280 feet or 1,609 meters (Blackcomb). The longest run is 11 kilometers (Peak to Creek, Whistler) and the highest lift goes up to 7,424 feet or 2,263 meters (Showcase T-Bar, Blackcomb).

The resort offers a wide range of terrain for skiers and snowboarders. Beginners can enjoy gentle slopes and dedicated learning areas, while more advanced skiers can tackle challenging steeps, couloirs, and glades. There are also two terrain and jump parks.

- **Whistler Blackcomb official website:** https://www. whistlerBlackcomb.com/
- **Whistler Blackcomb Trail Map:** https://www.whistlerBlackcomb. com/-/aemasset/sitecore/whistler-Blackcomb/maps/20221209_ Whistler Blackcomb_winter-trail_map_001.pdf
- **Whistler Blackcomb lift status:** https://www.whistlerBlackcomb. com/the-mountain/mountain-conditions/terrain-and-lift-status. aspx

WHISTLER MOUNTAIN

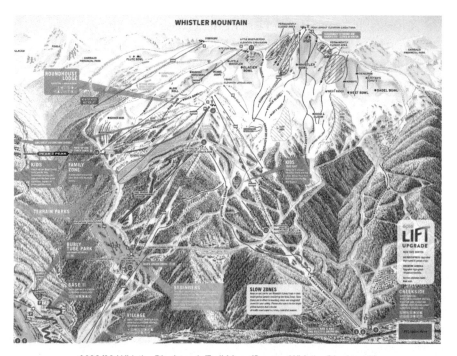

2022/23 Whistler Blackcomb Trail Map. (Source: Whistler Blackcomb)

Whistler Mountain is where skiing at Whistler Blackcomb originally started. In the early 1900s, the area was primarily used for logging and mining. In 1914, the railway was completed, providing access to the area and opening it up for tourism. In the 1920s, the first cabins were built in the Creekside area, and skiing and snowshoeing became popular winter activities. In the 1960s, the area was chosen as the site for a new ski resort, which was named Whistler Mountain. The ski resort officially opened on January 15, 1966, with a gondola and two double chairs, and quickly became popular with skiers and outdoor enthusiasts.

Today Whistler Mountain has 4,757 acres or 19.25 square kilometers of skiable terrain. It features a network of 100+ designated trails catering to all skill levels, ranging from gentle beginner slopes to challenging expert runs. Whistler Mountain is equipped with a comprehensive system of high-speed gondolas, chairlifts, and T-bars, ensuring quick and convenient access to the different areas on the mountain.

The Whistler side of Whistler Blackcomb can be broken down into several areas, including:

- Creekside Gondola and Big Red Express Chairlift
- Whistler Village Gondola and Fitzsimmons Chairlift (Fitz)
- Garbanzo Express Chairlift (Garbo)
- Emerald Express Chairlift (Green Chair)
- Peak Express Chairlift
- Harmony Express Chairlift
- Symphony Express Chairlift
- The Flute Bowls

Each of these areas has its own characteristics, benefits, and challenges.

NATURE NOTES

Hoary or Whistling Marmot

Whistler Mountain was originally known as 'London Mountain' and only officially became Whistler in 1965. The name was inspired by the whistling of the Hoary Marmots that are native to this area. These cute little rodents emit a high-pitched whistling noise as a warning. If you hike the alpine trails on Whistler or Blackcomb in the summer, you will often see these marmots and may hear their famous whistle!

Source: https://troymedia.com/travel/whistler-mountain-name-come-from/

Source: https://en.wikipedia.org/wiki/Hoary_marmot#/media/File:Marmota_caligata_(EH).jpg

WHISTLER MOUNTAIN

Creekside Gondola and Big Red Express Chairlift Area

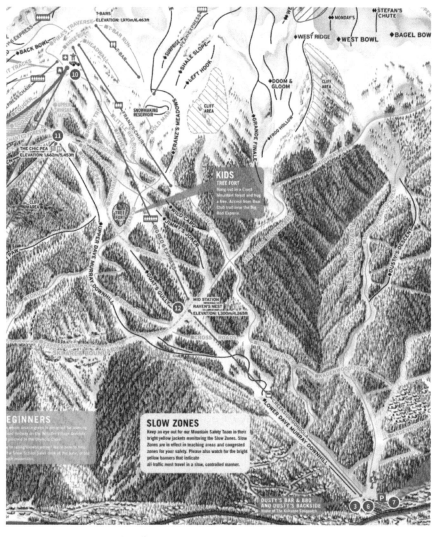

The Creekside and Big Red areas on Whistler.
(Source: 2022/23 Whistler Blackcomb Trail Map)

*T*he Creekside Gondola and Big Red Express Chairlift service the area located on the west side of Whistler Blackcomb and is the first part of the resort that you reach when driving in from Squamish and Vancouver. Whistler Creekside (the area at the base of this part of the resort) offers free underground day parking and is very popular with locals coming in to ski for the day. The Creekside Gondola runs up from Creekside and ends at the base of the Big Red Express Chairlift, which then runs up to end near the Roundhouse Lodge area.

From the top of the Creekside Gondola, you can access the Blue and Black runs back down to the Creekside base. There is also the Expressway run (Green) that takes you over to the Garbanzo Express Chairlift base and the Olympic Mid Station area.

From the top of the Big Red Express Chairlift, you can access:

- The Roundhouse Lodge
- Runs over to the Peak Express Chairlift
- Runs over to the T-Bar
- Runs over to the Harmony Express Chairlift base
- Runs down to the bottom of the Emerald Express Chairlift

There are a good variety of Green, Blue, and Black Runs (and even a Double-Black-like run) on this side of Whistler Mountain, making it a good area for beginners, intermediate and expert skiers, and snowboarders. This area is also home to the Whistler Tree Fort for younger kids. The Tree Fort can be accessed from either Bear Cub or Pony Trail (both Greens).

Locals' Tips

- If the rest of Whistler is busy, this area is worth considering for mid and lower mountain laps.
- If the lower mountain is icy or has not had much snow, it is sometimes a good idea to download via the Creekside Gondola versus skiing out to the Creekside base.
- Franz's Run can get skied out and icy towards the end of day. Other options are to take Bear Cub (Green) or Pony Trail (Green) down to the Big Red Express Chairlift base area.
- On a fresh snow/powder day, before the high mountain areas open, good powder run options include CC, Pale Face, and

Franz's Meadows. On the way up Big Red Express, keep watch for where people are skiing off-piste powder lines.

Gondolas/Lifts

Big Red Express Chairlift: This is the six-person chairlift that runs from the top of the Creekside Gondola up to just above the Roundhouse Lodge area.

Creekside Gondola: This is the eight-person gondola that runs from the Whistler Creekside base up to the base of Big Red Express Chairlift. The Creekside Gondola is the only access point up to Whistler Mountain from the Creekside base.

Franz's Chairlift: This is the older three-person chairlift that runs below and to the right of the Big Red Express Chairlift. It is only occasionally open when there is a lot of traffic on the hill.

Riding up the Big Red Express Chairlift on a fresh snow day.
(Source: Dan Bouthillette)

Lodges/Huts

The Raven's Nest: This is a small hut at the base of the Big Red Express Chairlift. It offers coffee, pastries, and a limited set of lunch options. The Raven's Nest has a small outdoor patio with views of the valley below (a beautiful spot on a sunny, warm afternoon). There are also washrooms in the basement of the building.

The Roundhouse Lodge: This is the main lodge on Whistler Mountain. It offers a cafe and two cafeterias, one on the top level and one on the lower level. It also contains Seppo's Bar and Steeps Grill and Wine Bar (reservations recommended). There are two outdoor patios, with one facing the mountain and one facing the valley. The famous Umbrella Bar sits on the very edge of the valley-side patio and offers great views of the valley. There are large men's and women's washrooms as well as two shops on the lower level.

Main Routes

● **Pony Trail – Expressway:** This is the main Green route on this side of Whistler Mountain. Pony Trails starts below the Roundhouse Lodge on the side towards the Big Red Express Chairlift and curves back and forth down to the Big Red Express Chairlift base. Expressway runs from the Big Red Express Chairlift base over to the Whistler Village side of the mountain and to Garbanzo Express Chairlift base.

> **NOTE:** There is no Green run down to the Creekside base from the top of the Creekside Gondola.

■ **CC – Fisheye/Little Red – Porcupine – Franz's – Lower Franz's:** This is the main Blue route from the Roundhouse Lodge down to the Creekside base. CC starts just below the Roundhouse Lodge and has several paths that lead down to the start of Fisheye and Little Red. Fisheye and Little Red continue down to join with Porcupine, which leads to the top of Franz's Run. Franz's runs down to Highway 86 and then becomes Lower Franz's Run, which leads down to Creekside base.

♦ **Upper and Lower Dave Murray Downhill:** This is the main Black route from the Chickpea Hut area down to the Creekside base. Upper Dave Murray starts just below the top of the Garbanzo Express Chairlift and runs down to Expressway (Green). On the other side of Expressway, it becomes Lower Dave Murray Downhill, which runs down to connect with Lower Franz's Run and continues down to the Creekside base.

Green Runs

Bear Cub: Bear Cub is a long, flat Green run that leads from the Franz's Chairlift base area across the side of the mountain and then zigzags down to the bottom of the Big Red Express Chairlift. Bear Cub has a long flat section between Banana Peel (Blue) and where it crosses Pony Trail (Green), so either pick up some speed or be prepared to pole your way across this stretch. For younger kids, Bear Cub also provides access to one side of the Whistler Tree Fort.

Expressway: Expressway is a relatively flat Green run that provides an exit from the top of the Creekside Gondola or Big Red Express Chairlift base over towards the Olympic Mid Station area and the Garbanzo Express Chairlift base.

Papoose: Papoose is a Green run from the Chickpea Hut area towards the top of Franz's Run (Blue).

Pony Trail: Pony Trail is the main Green run that curves from the Roundhouse Lodge area down to the Big Red Express Chairlift base. Below the Roundhouse Lodge there are several possible initial routes to follow down, some shorter and a bit steeper, some longer and less steep. For kids, Pony Trail provides access to the other side of the Whistler Tree Fort.

NOTE: The section from Bear Cub to Highway 86 is fairly steep and can be icy at the end of the day.

HISTORY NOTES

Roundhouse Lodge

The Roundhouse Lodge was originally a much smaller, hexagonal building perched on Whistler Mountain in a similar location to the current lodge. The first lodge was built in 1966 and opened in the following winter. It was a copy of a building in California, designed with a huge fireplace in the middle that skiers could use to warm themselves. Initially, there were no washrooms, and skiers had to use outhouses on the hill below the lodge. In the first season, hot drinks, soup, and sandwiches were served off a picnic table using a Coleman camp stove in the 'Red Shack' at the top of the Big Red Express Chairlift. In 1998, the original lodge was replaced with the current Roundhouse Lodge that we know today.

Source: https://blog.whistlermuseum.org/2015/05/09/what-is-round-about-the-roundhouse-lodge/

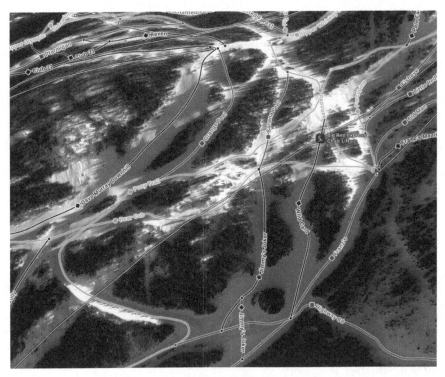

Green runs below the Big Red Express Chairlift.
(Source: FATMAP.com)

● **Upper Whiskey Jack:** Upper Whiskey Jack is a Green trail that runs from below the Roundhouse Lodge down to the Chickpea Hut area. It connects with Papoose, which leads down into the Big Red Express Chair area.

> **NOTE:** The run can be quite busy with beginners, as it is the easiest Green run below the Roundhouse Lodge.

Whistler Tree Fort: The Whistler Tree Fort is a kids' fort that sits in the forest between Bear Cub (Green) and Pony Trail (Green). The fort has different sections, some bridges, and some slides for kids to explore. On the Pony Trail side you will see a sign that clearly marks the path to the fort on the left side (looking downhill) of the run. This path leads to the fort and then back out again to Pony Trail. On the Bear Cub side, the entrance to the fort is also clearly marked on the right side (looking downhill) of the run and through a small tunnel. Many people leave their skis on the side of the run and walk through the tunnel to the fort area.

NOTE: There are no washrooms at the fort, so keep that in mind for your kids. The nearest washrooms would be down at the Raven Hut next to the base of the Big Red Express Chairlift.

Whistler Kids' Tree Fort on a fresh snow day.
(Source: Jaye Block)

Blue Runs

Banana Peel: Banana Peel is a short Blue run from the Chickpea Hut area that crosses Pony Trail (Green) and ends at Bear Cub (Green). If you continue straight across Bear Cub, this run turns into Jimmy's Joker (Black).

Crossroads: Crossroads is a narrow Blue run that leads from Expressway (Green) under the Creekside Gondola and over to connect with Lower Franz's Run (Blue).

Fisheye: Fisheye is a short, steep Blue run from Pony Trail (Green) to Papoose (Green). Papoose then runs to the top of Franz's run (Blue).

NOTE: There is a dip at the bottom of this run, so maintain your speed to get up the hump to the top of Franz's Run.

NATURE NOTES

Canada Jay or Whiskey Jack

The Canada Jay (perisoreus canadensis), also known as the Gray Jay, Gray Jay, camp robber, or Whiskey Jack, is found in boreal forests of North America north of the tree line, and in the Rocky Mountains subalpine zone south to New Mexico and Arizona.

Whiskey Jacks live year-round on permanent territories in coniferous forests, surviving in the winter months on food cached throughout their territory. They adapt to human activity and are known to approach humans for food, inspiring colloquial names including 'camp robber'. Although it is tempting to feed these friendly birds, please do not feed them, as human food can make them ill and feeding them can negatively affect their food-gathering habits.

In 2016, an online poll and expert panel conducted by *Canadian Geographic* magazine selected the Canada Jay as the national bird of Canada, although the designation is not yet formally recognized.

Source: https://en.wikipedia.org/wiki/Canada_jay

Owen Jones Cree with a Whiskey Jack on his head.
(Source: Nick Jones)

■ **Franz's Run:** Franz's run is a steep Blue run from Franz's Chairlift base down towards Highway 86 (Blue). You can turn right onto Highway 86 and head to the Big Red Express Chairlift base, or you can continue across Highway 86 and go down Lower Franz's Run (Blue). If you have kids (or are young at heart yourself), there is a short tunnel on the right side (looking downhill) of Highway 86 that is fun to ski through!

■ **(Lower) Kadenwood Trail:** Lower Kadenwood Trail is a long, narrow connector Blue run that starts on the left side (looking downhill) of Lower Dave Murray Downhill (Black), crosses Lower Franz's (Blue) and Lower Peak to Creek (Blue), and runs over to the Kadenwood neighborhood.

■ **(Upper) Kadenwood Trail:** Similar to Lower Kadenwood Trail (Blue), Upper Kadenwood Trail is a narrow connector Blue run that starts on the left side (looking downhill) of Lower Kadenwood Trail (Blue), crosses Lower Peak (Blue), and runs over to the Kadenwood neighborhood.

■ **Little Red Run:** Little Red Run is a short, steep Blue run from Pony Trail (Green) down to end on Fisheye. Fisheye connects with Papoose (Green) that then runs over to the top of Franz's Run (Blue).

  NOTE: At the bottom of this run there is a dip so keep up your speed to get up the hump to the top of Franz's run.

■ **Lower Franz's**: Lower Franz's runs from Highway 86 (Blue) down to the Creekside base. The center of the run is normally groomed, and there are ungroomed bumpy areas on either side of the run. Lower Franz's Run has both flatter and steeper sections. With fresh snow, this run can be quite fun.

  NOTE: At the end of day, Lower Franz's Run can be quite busy, as everyone is getting off the hill. Given its location lower on the mountain and due to heavy traffic, it may also become icy and bumpy.

■ **Old Man:** Old Man is an ungroomed, bumpy Blue run from the Peak Express Chairlift base around both sides of the snowmaking water reservoir down towards the top of Franz's Run (Blue).

  NOTE: At the bottom of this run, you need to pick up some speed to go up and over a small hump before the top of Franz's Run.

View from the Chickpea Hut area down into the valley past Creekside.
(Source: Nick Jones)

Orange Peel: Orange Peel is a short Blue run from the top of the Garbanzo Express Chairlift that meets with Pony Trail (Green) and then continues to end on Upper Dave Murray Downhill (Black).

Tokum: Tokum is a Blue that starts on the right side (looking downhill) of the Dave Murray Downhill (Black) and runs over to the Garbanzo Express Chairlift base area. Tokum can be a bit bumpy if it has not been groomed in a while but otherwise is a nice carvy Blue run.

Black Runs

♦ **Bear Paw:** Bear Paw is a steep Black run that starts off the right side (looking downhill) of Upper Dave Murray Downhill (Black) and runs down to the Garbanzo Express Chairlift base. Normally groomed, it can become quite bumpy with use. It can be a fun powder run and can have some great bumps and steep sections.

NOTE: Bear Paw is often in the shade and can get quite icy during spring from thaw/freeze cycles.

The Blacks under the Big Red Express Chairlift: Goat's Gully, Jimmy's Joker, and Wild Card. (Source: FATMAP.com)

◆ **(Upper) Dave Murray Downhill:** Upper Dave Murray is a big, wide Black run that starts just below the top of the Garbanzo Express Chairlift and runs down to Expressway (Green), where it turns into the Lower Dave Murray Downhill (Black). Normally groomed, this run can get bumpy with use and/or due to lack of grooming. You can still see the starting gate for the 2010 Olympics Men's downhill race at the top of this run.

◆ **(Lower) Dave Murray Downhill:** Lower Dave Murray Downhill is a big, long Black run from Expressway (Green) all the way down to the Creekside base. The whole Dave Murray Downhill from top to bottom is a classic, fun run, especially with good or fresh snow. You can live your Olympic dreams and try running it from top to bottom— but be warned, it is a thigh burner!

> **NOTE:** Because of its location lower down on the mountain, Lower Dave Murray Downhill can suffer from thaw/freeze cycles and become hard and icy. Depending upon the conditions, it can make more sense to download on the Creekside Gondola than to ski out via this run.

♦ **Goat's Gully:** Goats Gully is a steep, bumpy Black mogul run that drops from Bear Cub (Green) down to the bottom of the Big Red Express Chairlift. An earlier Whistler chairlift, called the Orange Chairlift, used to run up Goat's Gully and along the upper part of Upper Dave Murray Downhill.

> **NOTE:** This is a rugged, steep run. I recommend only approaching it when there is sufficient snow coverage.

♦ **Franz's Meadows:** Franz's Meadow is a small, ungroomed Black bowl below the ridge that includes Air Jordan and Waterfall Cliffs. You can access this bowl by following Old Man (Blue) around the top of the snowmaking reservoir and then traversing along under the cliffs. Once you are above the bowl, you can then drop into it and come out through the glades at the bottom near the top of Franz's Run (Blue). This bowl is a locals' favorite for fresh tracks on a powder day.

♦ **Jimmy's Joker:** Jimmy's Joker is a short, steep Black mogul run between Bear Cub (Green) at the top and Highway 86 (Blue) at the bottom. The run gets its name from a logger named Jimmy who accidentally cut it on a foggy day when he was actually supposed to be working on Franz's run.

♦ **Wildcard:** Wildcard is a steep Black mogul run between Bear Cub (Green) at the top and Highway 86 (Blue) at the bottom. This run was where the women's alpine downhill races would start during the 2010 Olympics.

Other Black Areas

♦ **CC:** CC is a set of short, ungroomed, and bumpy Black runs behind and below the Roundhouse Lodge and to the left (looking downhill) of the Whistler Village Gondola. All the CC runs end on Pony Trail (Green). If you are first on the hill on a powder day, the CC runs are worth trying for fresh tracks.

♦♦ **Insanity:** Insanity is not a marked run on Whistler, and the name is very appropriate. The top part runs down from Pony Trail (Green) under the Big Red Express Chairlift to the Big Red Express Chairlift Base. The lower half of Insanity runs from the top of the Creekside Gondola down under the Gondola, crosses Crossroads (Blue), and ends down on the Dave Murray Downhill run (Black).

NOTE: This is a very difficult, expert run with steep drops, exposure, and bumps. Due to its location on the mountain, this slope can have limited snow coverage. Do not attempt this run if it has been roped off by the ski patrol (you risk losing your pass if you are caught doing this).

♦ **Paleface:** Paleface is a short, bumpy run similar to CC (Black) that can be accessed below and behind the Roundhouse Lodge and under the Whistler Village Gondola. It ends on Pony Trail (Green). This is another run worth trying at the start of the day when there has been fresh snow.

HISTORY NOTES

Dave Murray Downhill

Dave Murray is one of Whistler's greatest skiing legends. Born and raised in Vancouver, his family owned a cabin on Alpha Lake, so Whistler was literally a second home. Dave's skiing earned him a spot on the legendary Crazy Canucks, a team of Canadian downhill racers in the late 1970s and early 1980s known for their fearless racing style. Fellow Crazy Canuck, Steve Podborski, remembers, 'Dave was a much more complex man than just a ski racer. He was a deep thinker who realized skiing was just for the moment. He was a powerful influence on all of us. He gave us a balance and perspective we wouldn't have had without him. He was a creator.'

Murray retired from competitive skiing following the 1982 season and returned to Whistler to set up the Dave Murray Ski School. He passed away in 1989, and the Downhill course was named in his honor in 1990. The run is considered one of the best in the world, and in 2010, the Dave Murray Downhill was used in the 2010 Winter Games.

Source: https://www.whistler.com/blog/post/2015/02/27/whats-in-a-name-whistler-mountain-ski-runs/

Whistler Village Gondola Mid Station and the Fitzsimmons Chairlift Area

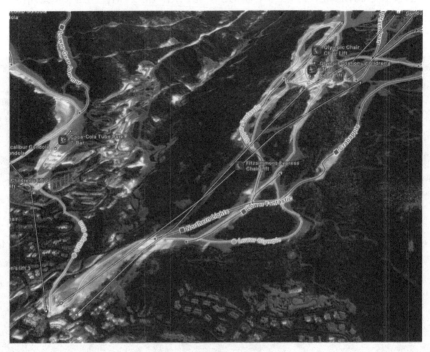

The Lower Whistler Gondola and Fitzsimmons area of Whistler.
(Source: FATMAP.com)

The Whistler Village Gondola and Fitzsimmons Express Chairlift are located on the lower part of Whistler, immediately above Whistler Village. This gondola and lift provide the two ways to upload onto Whistler Mountain from the village area. The Whistler Village Gondola runs up to the Olympic Mid Station and then continues up to the top next to the Roundhouse Lodge. The Fitzsimmons Chairlift runs up to the same lower mid mountain area as the Olympic Mid Station. There are a limited set of Blue and Green runs in this area that lead down to the Whistler Village base.

This area is mostly used by skiers and snowboarders to exit from the mountain down into the village. There is also a large beginner/learning zone situated uphill from the Olympic Mid Station, making it a great area for people learning how to ski and snowboard. The learning zone is serviced by the Olympic Chairlift as well as several magic carpet lifts for beginners.

Locals' Tips

- If the Whistler Village Gondola is busy, avoid the lineups and take the Fitzsimmons Chairlift up, then get onto the Garbanzo Express Chairlift to continue up the mountain.
- If the lower mountain is icy, consider downloading on the Whistler Village Gondola from the Roundhouse Lodge.
- In the spring, watch for big mounds of corn snow in the last section of Lower Olympic just above the Whistler Village base. You don't want to crash in front of the après-ski crowds at the GLC, Longhorn, and Dubh Linn Gate (restaurants / bars at the village base area)!
- If you want to do big laps in the afternoon, take the Whistler Village Gondola up and then ski down all the way to the Whistler Village base. Then get back on the gondola to head up again.

Gondolas/Lifts

Fitzsimmons Express Chairlift: This is the new eight-person chairlift that runs up from the Whistler Village base to the Olympic Mid Station area.

Olympic Chairlift: This is the short three-person chairlift that services the beginner/learning zone uphill from the Olympic Mid Station.

Whistler Village Gondola: This is the eight-person gondola that runs up from the Whistler Village base to the Roundhouse Lodge. The gondola stops at the Olympic Mid Station, where you can enter and exit. The Mid Station area is a learning area for kids and beginners.

Lodges/Huts

Ollie's Grilled Cheese Shack: This is a small food shack next to the Olympic Mid Station. It offers hot sandwiches, snacks, and drinks. There are no washrooms, and seating is outdoors only.

> **NOTE:** This shack may or may not be open and it is unclear if the resort plans to continue to operate it.

The other buildings in this area are the Olympic Mid Station building and some buildings used by the Whistler Blackcomb Ski School.

Main Routes

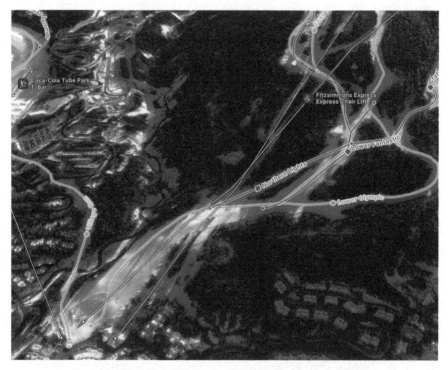

Blue and Green runs on the lower part of Whistler just above the village.
(Source: FATMAP.com)

⬤ **Lower Olympic:** This is the main Green run that leads out of the Olympic Mid Station area down to the Whistler Village base. It can get very busy at the end of the day, as everyone uses this run and Crabapple (Blue) to ski out to the Whistler Village base.

Heading down towards Whistler Village. Blackcomb Base and the Fairmont Hotel are in the background. (Source: Talia Polino)

■ **Lower Fantastic:** This is the main Blue run that leads down out of the Whistler Village Gondola Mid Station area to the Whistler Village base.

NOTE: Depending on the conditions, Lower Fantastic is sometimes closed for use.

There are no Black runs in this area.

Green Runs

● **Fitz:** Fitz is a short Green trail that runs from behind the top of the Fitzsimmons Express Chairlift to join with Lower Olympic (Green).

● **Lower Olympic:** Lower Olympic is the main Green run down to the Whistler Village base. It is wide, easy, and groomed.

NOTE: At the end of day, this run can be quite busy, as everyone is getting off the hill and snow conditions may be icy/difficult given the volume of skiers going down this run. In the spring, this part of the run can have lots of corn snow on it.

Blue Runs

■ **Crabapple:** Crabapple is a Blue run that goes down from Expressway (Green) past the top of the Fitzsimmons Express Chairlift to connect with Lower Olympic (Green). If you are coming down Expressway and want to head to the Whistler Village base, this is the route to follow.

■ **Lower Fantastic:** Lower Fantastic is a short Blue run that starts on Lower Olympic (Green) and then runs down to end on Lower Olympic, cutting the corner of the big elbow turn Lower Olympic makes towards the left (looking downhill).

NOTE: Depending on the conditions, Lower Fantastic is sometimes closed for use.

Garbanzo Express Chairlift Area

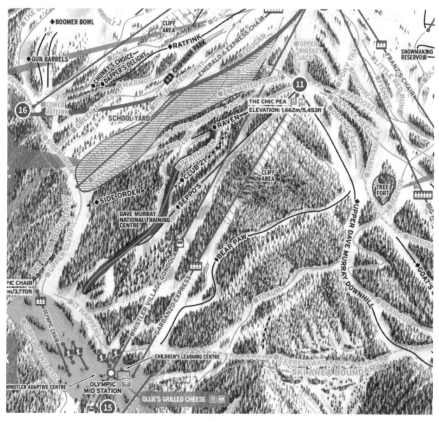

The Garbanzo area of Whistler.
(Source: 2022/23 Whistler Blackcomb Trail Map)

The Garbanzo Express Chairlift is located above the Olympic Mid Station area and below the Emerald Express Chairlift area on the front side of Whistler. This chairlift runs from the Olympic Mid Station area and the top of Fitzsimmons Chairlift up to the Chickpea Hut area.

At the top of the Garbanzo Express Chairlift you can:

- Ski down to Chickpea Hut.
- Access runs that go down to the bottom of the Emerald Express Chairlift and/or continue down to the Garbanzo Express Chairlift base or the Whistler Village base.
- Access runs down to the Big Red Express Chairlift base and/or continue down to the Creekside base.

This area offers a good combination of Green, Blue, and Black runs for all levels of skiers and snowboarders. The Chickpea Hut near the top of the Garbanzo Express Chairlift is a small, cozy hut that offers limited food and drinks, bench-style seating, and washrooms.

Looking towards the top of the Garbanzo Express Chairlift with The Saddle in the background. (Source: Nick Jones)

Gondolas/Lifts

Garbanzo Express Chairlift: Often referred to as just 'Garbo', this is the four-person chairlift that runs from the top of the Fitzsimmons Chairlift/Olympic Mid Station area up to just above the Chickpea Hut area. If there is ski-racing training happening, this is the lift that the young ski racers take to get back up to the top of the training courses located in this area.

Locals' Tips

- If the Whistler Village Gondola is busy, you can take the Fitzsimmons Chairlift up and then get onto the Garbanzo Express Chairlift to continue upward to avoid the Whistler Village Gondola lineups.
- If the rest of the mountain is getting busy, this whole front-side area is a good option to consider, as it will often have shorter wait times for lifts after 11 am.
- If you're planning a big vertical day, doing laps around the Garbanzo Express Chairlift (either down Upper Olympic or down Dave Murray Downhill and Tokum) is local skiers' favorite way to chalk up 50,000+ feet vertical days.

Lodges/Huts

Chickpea Hut: Chickpea Hut is a nice, small hut that offers food, seating, and washrooms. It is reminiscent of how ski lodges used to be with long tables and bench seating. Foodwise, it is known for its Big Hot Beef Dog with all the trimmings. In the spring, it has a nice small outside seating area where you can enjoy the warm weather. Chickpea is often where the kids ski-racing teams hang out, and it can be quite busy at those times.

Chickpea Hut on a sunny spring day with skiers and boarders enjoying lunch outside.
(Source: Nick Jones)

Main Routes

● **Lower Whiskey Jack – Upper Olympic – It Happens:** This is the main Green route in this area. When you get off the top of the Garbanzo Express Chairlift, ski straight ahead and down to Lower Whiskey Jack (Green). Ski down Lower Whiskey Jack to Upper Olympic (Green) and follow that down towards the Olympic Mid Station area. Above the Olympic Mid Station is a confusing mix of runs, so stay to the left and exit Upper Olympic onto It Happens (Green), which leads down towards the Garbanzo Express Chairlift. Follow the path that forks off over and down to the Garbanzo Express Chairlift base.

There are no Blue runs connecting into this area.

◆ **Upper Dave Murray – Bear Paw:** This is the main Black route in this area. When you get off the top of the Garbanzo Express Chairlift, go down to your right (looking downhill) to the start of Upper Dave Murray (you can still see the starting gate building from the 2010 Olympics at the top of this run). Take Upper Dave Murray down to the top of Bear Paw (Black) and then Bear Paw down to the Garbanzo Express Chairlift base area.

Green Runs

● **Bear Cub:** Bear Cub is a long, flat Green run that leads from the Franz's Chairlift base area across the side of the mountain and then zigzags down to the Big Red Express Chairlift base area. Bear Cub has a long flat section between Banana Peel (Blue) and where it crosses Pony Trail (Green), so either pick up some speed or be prepared to pole your way across this stretch. Just past the flat section, you will see the entrance to the Whistler Tree Fort for kids on the right. Bear Cub is mostly flat but does have a couple of tighter, slightly steep sections.

● **Expressway:** Expressway is a medium-wide Green run that provides a route from the top of the Creekside Gondola/Big Red Express Chairlift base over towards the Garbanzo Express Chairlift base/Olympic Mid Station area.

● **It Happens:** It Happens is a short, wide Green run that forks left (looking downhill) from Upper Olympic (Green) towards the Olympic Mid Station area and then reconnects with Upper Olympic to continue down to the Whistler Village base.

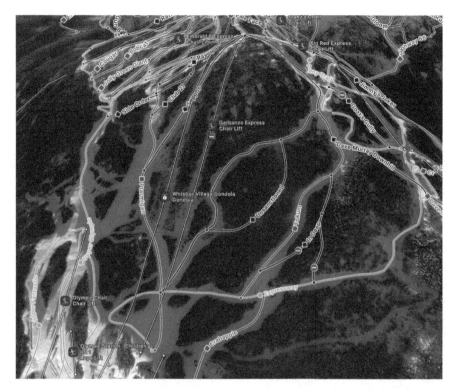

The Green runs that come down on either side of the Garbanzo Express Chairlift area. (Source: FATMAP.com)

● **Lower Whiskey Jack:** Lower Whiskey Jack is a long, wide Green run leading down from the Chickpea Hut area to connect with Upper Olympic (Green) near the Emerald Express Chairlift base.

● **Papoose:** Papoose is a short Green run from the Chickpea Hut area over towards the top of Franz's Run (Blue).

● **Pony Trail:** Pony Trail is the main Green run that curves down from the Roundhouse Lodge area to the Big Red Express Chairlift base. There are several possible initial routes to follow down from below the Roundhouse Lodge, some shorter and a bit steeper, some longer and less steep. For kids, Pony Trail provides another access point to the Whistler Tree Fort.

NOTE: The section from Bear Cub to Highway 86 (Blue) is fairly steep and can get icy at the end of the day due to skier traffic.

● **Upper Olympic:** Upper Olympic is the big, wide main Green run from the Emerald Express Chairlift base down to the Olympic Mid station area, where it connects with Lower Olympic (Green) that leads into the village.

> **NOTE:** At the end of the day, this run can get busy and skied out (icy, etc.), as many people use it to exit the upper mountain area.

HISTORY NOTES

Pony Trail

Pony Trail is the oldest run on Whistler Mountain. When the ski hill was being built in the summer of 1965, workers would take materials and supplies up the mountains by pack horse (called ponies). The pony trail of old was the route cut for the horses to use to get up the mountain. Because it followed the easiest route possible for the horses, it was the perfect candidate to become Whistler's first Green run.

Source: https://www.whistler.com/blog/post/2015/02/27/whats-in-a-name-whistler-mountain-ski-runs/

Blue Runs

■ **Banana Peel:** Banana Peel is a short Blue run from the Chickpea Hut area down to Pony Trail (Green) and then ends at Bear Cub

(Green). If you continue across Bear Cub, this run turns into Jimmy's Joker (Black).

■ **Old Crow:** Old Crow is a short Blue run from Raven (Black) across Ptarmigan (Blue) and down to connect with Lower Whiskey Jack (Green).

> **NOTE:** This run is sometimes closed off to the public when it is being used for skiing racing practice and/or events.

■ **Orange Peel:** Orange Peel is a short Blue run from the top of the Garbanzo Express Chairlift, down to Pony Trail (Green) and then ends on Upper Dave Murray Downhill (Black).

■ **Ptarmigan:** Ptarmigan is a long Blue run from Lower Whiskey Jack (Green) down to the Garbanzo Express Chairlift base area.

> **NOTE:** The top two thirds of this run is sometimes closed off to the public when used for skiing racing practice and events. The lower third is normally ungroomed and bumpy.

■ **Tokum:** Tokum is a Blue run that starts on the right side (looking downhill) of Dave Murray Downhill (Black) and runs over to end on Expressway. Tokum can be a bit bumpy if it has not been groomed in a while, but otherwise it is a nice carvy Blue run.

Black Runs/Areas

♦ **Bear Paw:** Bear Paw is a Black run with steep sections that starts off on the right side (looking downhill) of Upper Dave Murray Downhill (Black) and runs down to Expressway (Green) just above the Garbanzo Express Chairlift base area. This run is groomed occasionally but can get bumpy with use (or lack of grooming). This is a locals' favorite when there is powder or other fresh snow.

> **NOTE:** Due to its position on the mountain, this run can suffer from thaw/freeze cycles and become very icy. Check it out from above on the Garbanzo Express Chairlift before going down it.

♦ **Club 21:** Club 21 is a bumpy Black glade area beside Raven (Black) and above Ptarmigan (Blue). You can access this glade on the left side of Raven (Black) and then exit onto Ptarmigan (Blue). Only think about doing this run if there is sufficient snow to cover the moguls in this glade. If you exit Club 21 and want to continue skiing glades, you can cross Ptarmigan and go down Side Order (Black) on the other side.

♦♦ **In Deep:** In Deep is a very difficult, bumpy Double-Black glade area with lots of challenging features. Expert locals ski this glade, but only in good snow conditions. You can access In Deep from the left side of Tokum (Blue) and exit either back onto Tokum or onto Expressway (Green) at the bottom of this glade area.

> **NOTE:** There is a significant risk of tree wells in this area, so make sure you have a safety whistle, ski with one or more friends, and ski with caution.

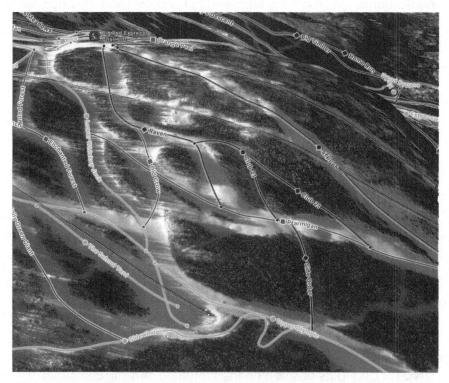

Some of the Blacks on the north side of the Garbanzo Express Chairlift area.
(Source: FATMAP.com)

♦ **Raven:** Raven is a short Black run immediately to the left (looking downhill) of the top of the Garbanzo Express Chairlift. It runs down to end on Ptarmigan (Blue).

♦ **Seppo's:** Seppo's is a long, bumpy Black with steep sections that runs from the top of the Garbanzo Express Chairlift down to Ptarmigan (Blue). Access this run by getting off Garbanzo, turning right, and skiing around under the lift towards the right. Below Ptarmigan there is a short Blue 'Lower Seppos' section that goes down to Upper Olympic.

NOTE: The top third of this run is quite flat before you hit the steep areas and requires a bit of work to get across.

HISTORY NOTES

Seppo Makinen

Seppo Makinen logged many of the early runs on both Whistler and Blackcomb. He was an unstoppable workhorse with incredible strength of body and character. In 1980, Seppo cut his last run, and the wild, off-camber descent quickly became a local's favorite on big snow days. It was named Seppo's in his honor.

Whenever nostalgia causes long-time Whistler locals to reminisce about the old days, the conversation invariably leads to Seppo, whose door was always open to those with nowhere else to stay. It says a lot about this community that one of the most cherished figures in our history was not a politician or founder in the traditional sense, but a generous and warm-hearted Finnish logger.

Source: https://www.whistler.com/blog/post/2015/02/27/whats-in-a-name-whistler-mountain-ski-runs/

◆ **Side Order:** Side Order a short, bumpy Black glade area below Ptarmigan (Blue) that runs down to Upper Olympic (Green). It basically continues from Club 21 (Black) above Ptarmigan. Trees on this run are well spaced, but moguls can be quite big. Only think of doing this run if there is sufficient snow to cover moguls in this glade.

◆ **Upper Dave Murray Downhill:** Upper Dave Murray is a big, wide Black run that starts just below the top of the Garbanzo Express Chairlift and runs down to Expressway (Green), where it turns into the Lower Dave Murray Downhill (Black). The Upper and Lower Dave Murray Downhill runs were used for the men's ski races during the 2010 Winter Olympics.

◆◆ **Unsanctioned:** Similar to In Deep (Black), Unsanctioned is a very difficult, bumpy Double-Black glade area with lots of challenging features, logs, and a creek to deal with. This run should only be attempted if there are good snow conditions. You can access

Unsanctioned from the left side of Bear Paw (Black) and exit back onto Bear Paw at the bottom of this run. Many locals consider this one of the worst runs in the whole resort area.

> **NOTE:** There is a significant risk of tree wells and creek holes in this area, so make sure you have a safety whistle, ski with one or more friends, and ski with caution!

Other Areas

■ **Garbanzo and Emerald Express Chairlift Bike Trails:** For children and families, a highlight of the Garbanzo Express Chairlift and Emerald Express Chairlift areas is the mountain bike trails. These mountain bike trails can be found all along Upper Whiskey Jack (Green) and Bear Cub (Green). They are smooth and flowy trails through the trees with banked corners. Some of the trails may have bumps that render them a darker shade of Blue. To find them, look for signs on the trees that the Whistler Ski School uses.

> **NOTE:** Always observe and follow any signage, as some bike trails may be closed (you risk losing your pass if you use them when they are closed).

◆ **Garbanzo Express Chairlift Line:** This is an unmarked Black 'run' under the Garbanzo Express Chairlift. It is ungroomed with big bumps, drops, cliffs, and steep sections. This run is a favorite with expert local skiers when there is fresh snow.

> **NOTE:** Do not attempt this run if it has been roped off by the ski patrol (you risk losing your pass if you are caught using a run when it is closed).

Looking down underneath the Whistler Village Gondola from Upper Whiskey Jack.
(Source: Nick Jones)

Emerald Express Chairlift Area

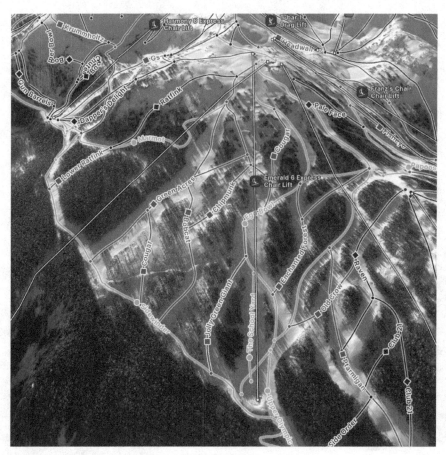

The Emerald Express Chairlift area of Whistler.
(Source: FATMAP.com)

The Emerald Express Chairlift area is located mid mountain, below the Roundhouse Lodge on Whistler. This area is accessible either via the Whistler Village Gondola or the Garbanzo Express Chairlift and is serviced by the Emerald Express Chairlift. This area offers a range of easier Green and Blue runs as well as some Black glade areas and is popular for beginner and intermediate skiers and snowboarders. This area is also popular with 'Park Rats' who want to ski the Whistler Terrain Park in this area.

From the top of the Emerald Express Chairlift, you can:

- Ski over to the Roundhouse Lodge.
- Ski over to the Peak Express Chairlift base.
- Access runs down to the bottom of the Harmony Express Chairlift.
- Access runs down to the Big Red Express Chairlift base.
- Access a variety of runs under and around the Emerald Express Chairlift.

NOTE: The Emerald Express Chairlift is the first lift to open up on Whistler in the morning, so most people do warm-up runs here at the start of the day. This chairlift is also the main lift used by the ski school. As a result, it can be quite busy at different times of the day.

Locals' Tips

- On a fresh snow/powder day, check out the glades between the runs, as they can be quite enjoyable (assuming you have the skill and experience to ski glades and off-piste).
- If the forecast suggests fresh snow the next day, think about buying a 'First Tracks' ticket. This will allow you to upload on the Whistler Village Gondola early, have breakfast at the top, and be amongst the first to get fresh tracks in the Emerald Express Chairlift area at the start of the day.

Gondolas/Lifts

Emerald Express Chairlift: This is the six-person, high-speed chairlift that services this area below the Roundhouse Lodge.

Lodges/Huts

Chickpea Hut: Chickpea Hut is a nice, small hut that offers food, seating, and washrooms. It is reminiscent of how ski lodges used to be with long tables and bench seating. It is known for its Big Hot Beef Dog with all the trimmings.

The Roundhouse Lodge: Roundhouse Lodge is the main lodge on Whistler Mountain. The lodge offers two cafes and two cafeterias, on the two levels. It also contains Seppo's Bar and a more formal restaurant called Steeps Grill and Wine Bar (reservations recommended). There are two outdoor patios, one facing the mountain and one facing the valley. The famous Umbrella Bar sits on the very edge of the valley-side patio and offers great views of the valley and surrounding mountains. There are large men's and women's washrooms as well as two shops on the lower level.

Roundhouse Lodge and the Peak 2 Peak Gondola shed seen from Ridge Run.
(Source: Nick Jones)

Main Routes

● **Ego Bowl:** This is the main Green route through the Emerald area. It starts below the Roundhouse Lodge and curves back and forth to end down at the bottom of the Emerald Express Chairlift.

■ **Jolly Green Giant:** This is the main Blue run down through the Emerald Express Chairlift area. It starts at the top of the Emerald Express Chairlift and runs down to end on Sidewinder (Green) just above the Emerald Express Chairlift base.

There is no Black run from the top to the bottom of the Emerald Express Chairlift area.

Green Runs

● **Ego Bowl:** Ego Bowl is a Green run from near the top of the Emerald Express Chairlift down to the bottom of the chairlift. The first half of Ego Bowl has some steep-ish sections (for beginners at least). The bottom of this run connects with Upper Olympic (Green), which continues down to the Olympic Mid Station area.

Ego Bowl run curving off the left and the Emerald Express Chairlift coming up on the right. (Source: Susan Rogers)

● **Lower Whiskey Jack:** Lower Whiskey Jack is wide Green run with some steeper sections that runs from the Chickpea Hut area down to connect with Upper Olympic (Green) near the bottom of the Emerald Express Chairlift.

● **Marmot:** Marmot is a Green run that leads from Jolly Green Giant (Blue) over to the bottom of the Harmony Express Chairlift. The bottom of this run ends on the flat area around the Harmony Express Chairlift Base, so it is important to pick up some speed to avoid having to walk/skate over to the chair.

NOTE: Although the lower part of this run is flat and easy, the first part of the run is narrow, quite steep, and more like a Blue run in terms of difficulty level.

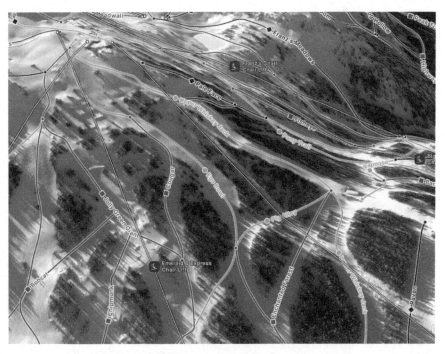

The Greens at the top of the Emerald Express Chairlift area:
Upper and Lower Whiskey Jack, Ego Bowl, and Pig Alley.
(Source: FATMAP.com)

● **Pig Alley:** Pig Alley is a short, easy Green run from the Chickpea Hut area over to the Ego Bowl run (Green).

HISTORY NOTES

Pig Alley

'Pig' was the nickname of the ski patrol's first Skidoo, a skidoo that often got stuck in the snow. The ski patrol had the Pig Alley trail cut because it was easier to cross over to Ego Bowl and climb that run than it was to climb Upper Whiskey Jack with their 'pig'.

Source: https://www.whistler.com/blog/post/2015/02/27/whats-in-a-name-whistler-mountain-ski-runs/

Example of an older Skidoo of the era of the Whistler Blackcomb Ski Patrol's first Skidoos. (Source: http://www.classicsledrestoration.com)

● **Sidewinder:** Sidewinder is a long, flat Green run from the bottom of the Harmony Express Chairlift over to the bottom of the Emerald Express Chairlift.

> **NOTE:** Sidewinder is quite flat and has some dips and humps. It is important to keep up your speed to avoid having to walk/skate up over the humps.

● **Upper Whiskey Jack:** Upper Whiskey Jack is a wide, easy Green run from below the Roundhouse Lodge down to the Chickpea Hut area. It connects with Lower Whiskey Jack (Green) to run down to the bottom of the Emerald Express Chairlift.

> **NOTE:** This section of Whiskey Jack can be very busy, as it is the easiest route from the Roundhouse Lodge area down to the Chickpea Hut area.

The School Yard in the Emerald area set up with a racecourse. (Source: Nick Jones)

● **The School Yard:** The School Yard is a short, wide Green that starts on the right side (looking downhill) of Ego Bowl (Green) and runs down to the bottom of the Emerald Express Chairlift.

NOTE: It is often used by the ski schools and is then closed off to the public.

Blue Runs

■ **Bobcat:** Bobcat is a Blue that starts on Jolly Green Giant (Blue) and runs through the Emerald Express Chairlift area. The top section includes jumps for the Whistler Terrain Park. The bottom section, past the terrain park, is ungroomed and includes a mogul section at the bottom where it ends on Sidewinder (Green). On a fresh snow day, this can be a fun run with fluffy bumps.

■ **Cougar Trail:** Cougar Trail is a short, bumpy Blue run with a steep-ish slope between Ego Bowl (Green) at the top and Jolly Green Giant (Blue) at the bottom.

■ **Coyote:** Coyote is a short, bumpy Blue run between Green Acres (Blue) at the top and Sidewinder (Green) at the bottom.

The bumpy bottom of Bobcat seen from Sidewinder on a bluebird-day morning.
(Source: Nick Jones)

Chipmunk: Chipmunk is a Blue run that starts on Jolly Green Giant (Blue) and ends on it again lower down the hill. This run is full of the various jumps and terrain features of the Whistler Terrain Park.

> **NOTE:** Before you go into a terrain park, read all the signs at the entrance to the park. Freestyle skiing comes with a greater risk, and you must understand what steps to take to make the park safe for you and everyone around you. If you are unsure, watch a video, ask an experienced rider, or consider booking a park lesson. For more information about terrain park safety, check out: https://www.whistlerblackcomb.com/the-mountain/more-options/safety.aspx

Enchanted Forest Run: The Enchanted Forest Run is a wide Blue run that starts below the Chickpea Hut and goes down to Ego Bowl (Green). Enchanted Forest has a secondary start at the bottom of Pig Alley (Green), which drops down to connect with the main run below. This run is groomed but can have bumps on it. It is a local favorite for a warm-up lap if there is fresh snow.

The Blues at the bottom of the Emerald Express Chairlift area: Green Acres, Chipmunk, Bobcat, Cougar, and Jolly Green Giant. (Source: FATMAP.com)

■ **Green Acres:** Green Acres is a big, wide Blue that runs from the right side (looking downhill) of Jolly Green Giant (Blue) below the top of the Emerald Express Chairlift and down to Sidewinder (Green) at the bottom. There is usually a groomed path down the middle of the run, with bumpy/ungroomed areas on either side.

■ **GS Run:** The GS Run is a Blue run from the top of the Emerald Express Chairlift down to the bottom of the Harmony Express Chairlift. This run has flatter and steeper sections with lots of ungroomed snow on either side. The first section is quite flat and even a bit uphill, so pick up some speed so you can get across it.

> **NOTE**: The bottom part of GS, below where it crosses Harmony Piste (Blue), is a steep Blue that can get icy and bumpy from heavy traffic.

■ **Jolly Green Giant:** Jolly Green Giant is the main, long Blue run from the top of the Emerald Express Chairlift down to Sidewinder (Green) near the bottom of the Emerald Express Chairlift. With steeper, flatter, and bumpy sections, it passes the Whistler Terrain Park and runs parallel with Ego Bowl (Green) for a short stretch.

■ **Lower Ratfink:** Lower Ratfink is the lower, Blue section below the bumpy Ratfink (Black) run above. It runs between Marmot (Green) at the top and Sidewinder (Green) at the bottom.

View from the Emerald Express Chairlift looking southeast towards Harmony Bowl on a bluebird day. (Source: Patrick Kolb)

Other Black Runs

◆ **Chunky's Choice:** Chunky's Choice is a well-known Black mogul run from GS Run (Blue) down to the bottom of the Harmony Express Chairlift. Chunky's Choice crosses Harmony Piste (Blue), which you can choose to take over to Sidewinder (Green). This is an expert run and for people who enjoy bumps. It is a favorite run for expert locals on the way over to Harmony Express Chairlift.

> **NOTE:** Chunky's Choice has big moguls, steep sections, and constriction points (where there may only be one or two ways to get down). Only consider doing this run if there is good snow to cover moguls on this run.

◆ **Dapper's Delight:** Dapper's Delight is a shorter, narrower version of Chunky's Choice (Black). It is a difficult, bumpy Black run that starts on the left side of Chunky's Choice about a third of the way down and then runs down to the Harmony Express Chairlift base. Dapper's Delight also crosses Harmony Piste (Blue) about halfway down.

> **NOTE:** Only consider doing this run if there is good snow to cover the moguls on this run.

The Blacks that sit between the Emerald Express Chairlift and Harmony Express Chairlift areas: Ratfink, Dapper's Delight, and Chunky's Choice. (Source: FATMAP.com)

◆ **Ratfink:** Ratfink is a Black mogul run with a steep, wide face at the top and a narrower exit at the bottom. To access Ratfink, start at the top of the Emerald Express Chairlift, head downhill for the ridge of trees halfway between Jolly Green Giant (Blue) on the left and GS Run (Blue) on the right. Ratfink starts on the other side of the ridge.

> **NOTE:** Similar to the other mogul runs in this area, only consider doing this run if there is good snow to cover the moguls on this run.

Other Areas

■ **Garbanzo and Emerald Express Chairlift Bike Trails:** For children and families, a highlight of the Garbanzo Express Chairlift and Emerald Express Chairlift areas is the mountain bike trails. These mountain bike trails can be found all along the Upper Whiskey Jack (Green) and Bear Cub (Green) runs. They are smooth and flowy trails through the trees with banked corners. Some of the trails may have bumps that render them a darker shade of Blue. To find them, look for signs on the trees that the Whistler Ski School uses.

NOTE: Always observe and follow any signage, as some bike trails may be closed (you risk losing your pass if you use them when they are closed).

◆ **Emerald Glades:** There are a variety of unmarked Black glades between most of the runs in the Emerald Express Chairlift area. Glades with more widely spaced trees can be found between Green Acres (Blue) and Cougar (Blue), between Cougar and Bobcat (Blue), and between Bobcat and Jolly Green Giant (Blue). Glades with trees that are closer together can be found between other runs in this area. After a good snow, these glades can be quite wonderful and are one of my personal favorites on Whistler.

■ **Whistler Terrain Park:** As you go up the Emerald Express Chairlift, you can see the Whistler Terrain Park below the lift to the left. This is a beginner-intermediate focused terrain park with beginner and intermediate sections. In the terrain park you will find jumps that range from three to ten-foot gaps and a range of rails and boxes (for more information, visit https://www.whistler.com/skiing/terrain-parks/). The Whistler Terrain Park is a great place to learn how to hit jumps and ski park style.

NOTE: Before you go into a terrain park, read all the signs at the entrance to the park. Freestyle skiing comes with a greater risk, and you must understand what steps to take to make the park safe for you and everyone around you. If you are unsure, watch a video, ask an experienced rider, or consider booking a park lesson. For more information about terrain park safety, check out: https://www.whistlerblackcomb.com/the-mountain/more-options/safety.aspx

■ / ◆ **Enchanted Forest Glades:** Enchanted Forest Glades is a glade area between Ego Bowl (Green) and Enchanted Forest (Blue). There are several paths cut through this area to allow kids to ski through the glades safely (Blue difficulty). The rest of the glade should be considered Black. The main entrance to the glades is identified by a wooden archway on the left side (looking downhill) of Ego Bowl.

◆ **Zudrell's:** Zudrell is an unmarked, bumpy Black run with trees and other terrain features that runs under the Peak 2 Peak Gondola from Marmot (Green) down to Sidewinder (Green). The story goes that Mathais Zudrell (a Doppelmayr engineer) was the first to ride across the Peak 2 Peak Gondola when it was constructed, so the run was named after him.

> **NOTE:** This is an expert run with big moguls, stumps, and trees. At the bottom, do not continue past Sidewinder, as this is out of bounds and leads to dangerous terrain and cliffs down to Fitzsimmons Creek (which will probably require a ski patrol rescue to get you out).

Max and Meredith Block about to enter the Enchanted Forest.
(Source: Jaye Block)

Peak 2 Peak crossing over the Emerald Express Chairlift above Ego Bowl with 7th Heaven in the background (Source: Nick Jones)

Peak Express Chairlift Area

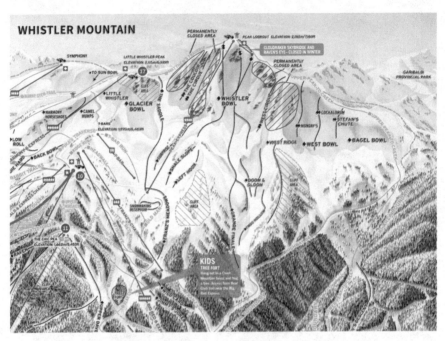

The Peak area of Whistler.
(Source: 2022/23 Whistler Blackcomb Trail Map)

The Peak Express Chairlift area includes Whistler Peak and is located above the Roundhouse Lodge, Big Red Express Chairlift, and Peak to Creek areas of Whistler. The Peak Express Chairlift takes you up to 7,160 feet or 2,182 meters at the top of Whistler Mountain and is considered one of the top chairlift experiences in the world. On a clear day, there are wonderful views of Black Tusk and the Coastal Mountain Range from the area at the top of the lift.

From the top of the Peak Express Chairlift, you can:

- Take Matthew's Traverse over to The Saddle (Black).
- Take Matthew's Traverse over to and then down Burnt Stew Trail (Green) into Symphony Bowl.

- Access Whistler Bowl (Black).
- Access West Bowl (Black) via Peak to Creek (Blue).
- Access Bagel Bowl (Black) via Peak to Creek (Blue).
- Access Peak to Creek (Blue), which runs down to either the Creekside base or back to the Big Red Express Chairlift via Highway 86 (Blue).

When standing in line for the Peak Express Chairlift, look up and to the right to see freeride 'rippers' showing their stuff and doing jumps off the Air Jordan and Waterfall cliff faces.

There are lots of Black and Double-Black runs and areas accessible from the top of the Peak Express Chairlift, including:

- Whistler Bowl run down to Grande Finale.
- West Bowl (expert zone) and its associated Black runs.
- Easier Bagel Bowl (great with fresh snow).

NOTE: The Peak Express Chairlift area is wonderful with good snow and visibility. With poor snow and visibility, it can be very difficult and even dangerous, given the difficulty of the runs and bowls in this area.

Locals' Tips

- If visibility or the weather conditions are poor, seriously consider skiing another part of the mountain and coming back to the Peak on a better day, unless you are very familiar with the Peak area.
- Bagel Bowl, West Bowl, and Whistler Bowl are north facing and so protected from the thaw/freeze cycles of south-facing slopes and bowls. As a result, there can be pockets of dryer snow here.
- If you are not familiar with the area, try to find someone who knows the runs and bowls to guide you through for the first couple of times. Some of the entrances, drops, and runs in this area are very gnarly!

Gondolas/Lifts

Peak Express Chairlift: This is the four-person, high-speed chairlift that provides access to Whistler Peak. This chair can be closed by Whistler Blackcomb when there are adverse weather conditions such as high winds.

T-Bar: This is the T-bar lift that runs from near the base of the Peak Express Chairlift up to the top of the ridge between Glacier Bowl and Harmony Bowl. It provides access down into Harmony as well as to the runs on either side of the T-bar back down into Glacier Bowl.

Lodges/Huts

There are no lodges or huts open to the public at the top of Whistler Peak.

Main Routes

● **Matthew's Traverse:** Matthew's Traverse is the only Green run at the top of the Peak Express Chairlift. It runs down from the top of the chairlift to the top of The Saddle (Black) on the left, or you can turn right and go down Burnt Stew Trail (Green) into Symphony Bowl.

■ **Upper Peak to Creek – Lower Peak to Creek:** This the main Blue route from the top of the Peak Express Chairlift. Take Upper Peak to Creek down to Lower Peak to Creek, then head down to the Creekside base.

■ **Upper Peak to Creek – Highway 86:** This the other main Blue route from the top of the Peak Express Chairlift. Take Upper Peak to Creek down to where Lower Peak to Creek forks to the left. Then take Highway 86 to the right to head back over to the Big Red Express Chairlift base.

◆ **Whistler Bowl – Grande Finale:** This is the main Black route down from the Peak. Enter Whistler Bowl and follow it down to Grande Finale (in the middle right bottom of the bowl). Grande Finale leads down to Highway 86, which then runs back to the Big Red Express Chairlift base.

Green Runs

● **Matthew's Traverse:** Matthew's Traverse is a flat, narrow Green that runs from the top of the Peak Express Chairlift over to the top of The Saddle (Black). From here, you can either turn left down The Saddle or you can turn right and go down Burnt Stew Trail (Green) into Symphony Bowl. On a clear day, this run offers amazing views of Black Tusk and the mountains of Coastal Mountain Range.

MOUNTAIN NOTES

Peak Express Chairlift

Ski Magazine asked skiers their opinions on the nine most iconic chairlift rides in North America and got oodles of replies.

Whistler's Peak Express Chairlift came in third and was described as: "The high-speed quad is the gnarliest lift on the mountain thanks to the 100-foot cliff just beneath the summit that it glides over, giving riders an up-close and personal view of the steep drops on offer. You also cruise over ancient glaciers and reward yourself with a magnificent 360° view from the summit, including a glacial lake. The terrain served is Black to Double-Black Diamond, including classic pods like Little Whistler Bowls and Surprise."

The Peak Express Chairlift is worth the ride, but hold on to your stomach as you pop over the top and get ready for a quick exit!

Source: https://www.skimag.com/ski-resort-life/9-most-iconic-chairlifts-north-america/

Looking up the Peak Express Chairlift and Whistler Peak on a bluebird day.
(Source: Nick Jones)

Blue Runs

■ **Highway 86:** Highway 86 starts at the bottom of Upper Peak to Creek (Blue) just below the tree line. It is a long, narrow Blue run with flatter sections that ends on Pony Trail (Green), which then runs down to the bottom of the Big Red Express Chairlift.

NOTE: This run and Pony Trail can be quite busy and congested, as they are some of the main routes out of the Peak area back down to the Big Red Express Chairlift.

■ **Ridge Run:** Ridge Run is a narrow Blue run across the ridge above and to the left (looking uphill) of the T-Bar, ending at the top of the Emerald Express Chairlift. It gives access to Headwall (Black), Jump Hill (Black), and several other short Black and Double-Black runs. The first part of Ridge Run is slightly uphill and requires skating or sidestepping to get up.

The Saddle running down into Glacier Bowl.
(Source: FATMAP.com)

■ **T-Bar Run:** The T-Bar Run is a wide Blue that runs down beside the T-Bar. It is normally groomed, but it can get bumpy with use. Originally, the T-Bars were the highest lifts on Whistler, and the T-Bar Run was the highest run you could access with a lift. If you take this T-Bar and ski this run, you are skiing a piece of Whistler history!

■ **Upper Peak to Creek:** Upper Peak to Creek is the first half of the long, steep Blue Peak to Creek run that drops from the top of Peak Express Chairlift all the way down to the Creekside base (an

11-kilometer/5,020-foot drop). Upper Peak to Creek starts at the top of the Peak Express Chairlift and ends just into the tree line. At the bottom of this run, you can either go down Lower Peak to Creek (Blue) to the Creekside base or take Highway 86 (Blue) over to the Big Red Express Chairlift base.

NOTE: Upper Peak to Creek is normally groomed but does get icy and bumpy with heavy use.

NATURE NOTES

Black Tusk

Black Tusk is a rock pinnacle that is the remnant of a volcano in Garibaldi Provincial Park of British Columbia, Canada. At 7,608 feet above sea level, the pinnacle is visible from a great distance in all directions. It is particularly noticeable from the Sea-to-Sky Highway just south of Whistler, British Columbia, as well as from Whistler Peak and the 7th Heaven area on Blackcomb. Very distinctive and unique, Black Tusk is arguably the best-known mountain in the Garibaldi Ranges of the Coast Mountains.

Source: https://en.wikipedia.org/wiki/The_Black_Tusk

A young Owen Jones Cree at the top of the Harmony Express Chairlift with Black Tusk in the background. (Source: Nick Jones)

Ripping down Upper Peak to Creek with Black Tusk in the background.
(Source: Helga Mepham)

Black Runs/Areas

NOTE: All the Black runs associated with the Peak Express Chairlift are expert runs. They include areas of ungroomed snow, steep sections, chutes, bumps, trees, and other challenging terrain.

Bagel Bowl

Bagel Bowl is the smallest and easiest of the Whistler Peak bowls and is located on the western edge of the Whistler Peak area.

♦ **Bagel Bowl:** Bagel Bowl is a relatively shallow, ungroomed, bumpy Black bowl on the western edge of the Peak Express Chairlift area. You can access it from the left side (looking downhill) of Upper Peak to Creek (Blue). You exit at the bottom of the bowl back onto Peak to Creek.

♦ **Bagel Roll:** Bagel Roll is a steep, Black slope to the right side (looking downhill) of Bagel Bowl (Black). You can access it from the right side (looking downhill) of Peak to Creek (Blue), and it exits down into the bottom of West Bowl (Black), which then leads down to Highway 86 (Blue).

♦ **Cream Cheese Ridge:** Cream Cheese Ridge (see the theme here?) is a steep, Black ridge run to the right of Bagel Roll (Black). You can access it from Peak to Creek, and it exits down into the bottom of West Bowl (Black), which then leads down to Highway 86 (Blue).

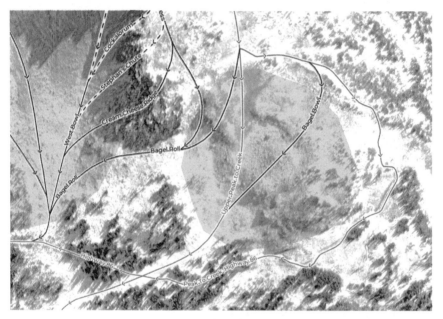

Bagel Bowl on the far west side of the Peak Express Chairlift area.
(Source: Openskimap.org)

Glacier Bowl

Glacier Bowl is the largest bowl below Whistler Peak and is located above and to the left (looking uphill) of the Peak Express Chairlift. The Saddle (Black) runs down into the middle of this bowl, and there are several Black and Double-Black runs along its edge.

♦ **East Ridge:** East Ridge is a Black run across the top of the ridge between Glacier Bowl and Whistler Bowl. You can access it from several points in Whistler Bowl, and it provides access to runs into the Whistler and Glacier Bowls.

♦ **Glacier Bowl:** There are a series of routes down the left side (looking uphill) of Glacier Bowl. These routes are all accessible from Jacob's Ladder (Black), which runs below Little Whistler Ridge.

♦ **Headwall:** Although shown on the Whistler Blackcomb Trail Map as a Blue, Headwall is really a short, steep Black wall that drops down from Ridge Run (Blue) and ends at the bottom of the T-bar. It is ungroomed and bumpy but can be great fun with good snow.

♦ **Left Hook:** Left Hook is the rightmost of the bumpy Black runs above and to the right (looking uphill) of the Peak Express Chairlift base area. It is accessible from East Ridge (Black) and runs down to the bottom of the Peak Express Chairlift. There are some small trees on the right side of the run, and it is also used by freeriders and rippers to access Waterfall Ridge (Double Black).

♦ **North Face:** North Face is a steep, bumpy Black run that curves down through a series of faces and cliffs below East Ridge (Black). It is accessible from East Ridge and ends down on The Saddle (Black).

♦ **Shale Chute:** Shale Chute is the narrow Black chute/gully on the left side (looking downhill) of Shale Slope (Black). It is accessible from East Ridge (Black) and runs down to the bottom of the Peak Express Chairlift.

♦ **Shale Slope:** Shale Slope is the wide, bumpy Black slope to the right (looking uphill) of the Peak Express Chairlift. It is accessible from East Ridge (Black) and runs down to the bottom of the Peak Express Chairlift. Shale Slope gets its name from the broken red shale (visible in the summer) that covers this slope.

♦ **Surprise:** Surprise is steep, bumpy Black run down the slope below The Coffin (Triple Black). It is accessible from either The Coffin or North Face (Black) and ends down on The Saddle (Black) that then continues down to the bottom of the Peak Express Chairlift.

♦♦ **The Cirque:** The Cirque is an extremely steep, difficult, Double-Black run that drops into the Glacier Bowl and ends down on The Saddle (Black). The entrance is accessible from Matthew's Traverse (Green) and is extremely narrow and rocky.

NOTE: This is an experts-only run and should only be attempted with caution. Even expert locals approach this run with extreme caution.

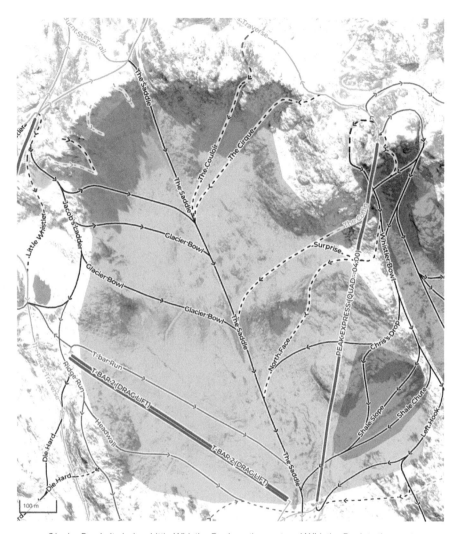

Glacier Bowl sits below Little Whistler Peak on the east and Whistler Peak to the west. (Source: Openskimap.org)

◆◆ The Couloir: The Couloir is the other extremely steep, difficult Double-Black run that drops into the Glacier Bowl and ends on The Saddle (Black). Similar to The Cirque (Double Black), this run is accessible from Matthew's Traverse (Green). Some locals have been heard to remark that it is amazing that this is a sanctioned run within Whistler Blackcomb given its extreme difficulty.

> **NOTE:** The entrance to this run is over a cornice and then onto an extremely exposed and rocky slope with cliffs on either side.

Many consider The Couloir to be the most difficult marked run in the entire Whistler Blackcomb Resort, and it has a worldwide reputation with expert skiers.

Three skiers contemplating the entrance into The Cirque! (Source: Jennifer Nairn)

♦ **The Saddle:** The Saddle is a big, wide, steep Black run that starts at the end of Matthew's Traverse (Green), goes down a steep section, and then runs to the bottom of the Peak Express Chairlift. Although it is regularly groomed, it can be icy, and the top third can turn into a mogul field with heavy use. There are mogul fields on either side of The Saddle that can be quite fun with good snow.

NOTE: Watch for huge chunks (some are the size of small cars) of avalanche debris from avalanche blasting on either side of The Saddle and avoid them if you go into this area.

West Bowl

West Bowl is a large Black bowl below and to the west of Whistler Peak. It is known for its Double-Black runs, steep lines, and powder snow.

◆ **Bonsai:** Bonsai is Black glade area that runs down from West Ridge (Black) down to end on Highway 86 (Blue). On a fresh snow day, many people consider this run and its neighbor —Everglades (Black)—to offer some of the finest steep, alpine glade skiing in all of Whistler Blackcomb.

> **NOTE:** This run starts in the open alpine and ends in the trees. When entering the tree line, exercise caution and watch for small trees that can catch your skis. When approaching the bottom of this area, watch for traffic as you enter Highway 86.

West Bowl sitting between Whistler Bowl to the east and Bagel Bowl to the west.
(Source: Openskimap.org)

♦♦ **Cockalorum:** Cockalorum is the second highest entrance into West Bowl and is a difficult, steep Double Black. The entrance to this run is accessible from Upper Peak to Creek (Blue), and it exits at the bottom through glades and mogul fields onto Highway 86 (Blue). Expert local skiers love to ski this run and West Bowl on powder days.

> **NOTE:** The entrance to this run is over the cornice that runs across the top of West Bowl. Depending on conditions, this can be easier or harder. Approach with caution!

♦ **Everglades:** Everglades is a Black glade area that runs from West Ridge (Black) down into West Bowl.

> **NOTE:** This run starts in the open alpine and ends in the trees. When entering the tree line, exercise caution and watch for small trees that can catch your skis.

◆◆ **Monday's:** Monday's is the highest entrance into West Bowl (Black) and is a difficult, steep Double-Black run. Similar to Cockalorum, you can access this run from Upper Peak to Creek, and it exits at the bottom through glades and mogul fields onto Highway 86 (Blue).

> **NOTE:** The entrance to this run is over the cornice that runs across the top of West Bowl. Depending on conditions, entering this run can be very challenging!

◆◆ **Stefan's Chute:** Stefan's Chute is a difficult, steep, narrow Double-Black chute on the left side (looking downhill) of West Bowl. You can access it from Upper Peak to Creek (Blue), and it ends into West Bowl.

> **NOTE:** As with the other West Bowl runs, the entrance is over the cornice, and expert skiing skills are required for this run.

Whistler Bowl

Whistler Bowl sits between Glacier Bowl in the east and West Bowl in the west. It is arguably the most famous of the three bowls, as it runs underneath the top part of the Peak Express Chair and offers access to a wide range of Black and Double Black runs. The top part of the bowl, underneath the chairlift, contains the remnants of the once mighty Whistler Glacier. This is a go-to area for locals on a fresh snow day.

◆◆ **Alley Bear:** Alley Bear is a steep Double-Black run down the right side (looking downhill) of Whistler Bowl (Black). It starts at the end of the East Ridge (Black) and runs down to Grande Finale (Black).

> **NOTE:** This run starts in the open alpine, drops down a steep face, and ends in the trees. When entering the tree line, exercise caution and watch for small trees that can catch your skis.

◆ **Doom and Gloom:** Doom and Gloom are two Blacks runs down the middle and side of the moraine near the bottom of Whistler Bowl. Doom runs down from the top of the moraine, and Gloom runs down the left side (looking downhill). Both are accessible from Whistler Bowl (Black), and both end on Grande Finale (Black).

> **NOTE:** The entire Whistler Bowl area is steep, ungroomed, and bumpy. Approach with caution.

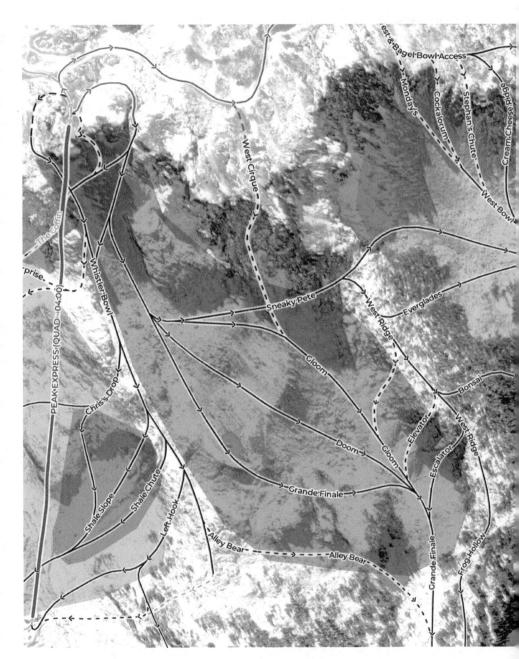

Whistler Bowl below Whistler Peak.
(Source: Openskimap.org)

◆◆ Elevator: Sunrise is a steep, difficult Double-Black chute that runs from West Ridge (Black) down into Whistler Bowl (Black).

> **NOTE:** This is a narrow, rocky chute and it should be approached with caution.

◆ Escalator: Escalator is a short, steep Black run that starts near the end of West Ridge (Black) and runs down into the bottom of Whistler Bowl, ending on Grande Finale (Black).

◆ Frog Hollow: Frog Hollow is an area of Black glade skiing that starts at the end of West Ridge (Black). You exit Frog Hollow at the bottom onto Highway 86 (Blue).

◆ Grande Finale: Grande Finale is a Black run that starts in the middle of Whistler Bowl and curves down to Highway 86 (Blue). This run provides the main exit out of the bottom of Whistler Bowl. This run can include areas of moguls, some flatter areas, and glade skiing towards the end of the run.

◆◆ Liftie's Leap: Liftie's Leap is a very steep, difficult Double-Black drop into Whistler Bowl. The entrance is over a cornice followed by a steep drop onto the glacier below.

> **NOTE:** This is a very challenging, difficult, and exposed drop that should only be attempted with great caution when snow conditions are good.

◆ Sneaky Pete: Sneaky Pete is a Black traverse run from Whistler Bowl over to West Ridge (Black). It gives access to West Bowl (Black) and West Ridge (Black).

◆◆ Sunrise: Sunrise is a steep, difficult Double Black that runs from West Ridge (Black) down into Whistler Bowl (Black).

◆◆ West Cirque: The West Cirque is an extremely steep, difficult Double-Black run that drops into and ends in Whistler Bowl. This run is accessible by following a path from Peak to Creek (Blue) to the edge of the bowl. The entrance to this run is a narrow rocky chute.

> **NOTE:** This is an experts-only run and should be attempted with extreme caution. Similar to The Cirque (Double Black) and the Couloir (Double Black), even expert locals approach this run with extreme caution.

♦ **West Ridge:** West Ridge is a Black run across the top of the ridge between Whistler Bowl and West Bowl. It starts from the Sneaky Pete traverse (Black) and runs along down the ridge to end at the top of Frog Hollow (Black). West Ridge provides access to a variety of Black and Double-Black runs on either side of the ridge.

> **NOTE:** Watch for and obey warning and cliff signs to avoid dangerous terrain.

♦ **Whistler Bowl:** Whistler Bowl has numerous routes down the middle and sides of the bowl leading down to Grande Finale (Black) or Doom and Gloom (Black).

♦♦ **Whistler Cornice:** Whistler Cornice is a steep, difficult Double-Black drop over a cornice into Whistler Bowl. It is accessible on the left at the top of the Peak Express Chairlift.

> **NOTE:** This is a very challenging, difficult, exposed drop and should only be attempted with great caution.

Other Areas

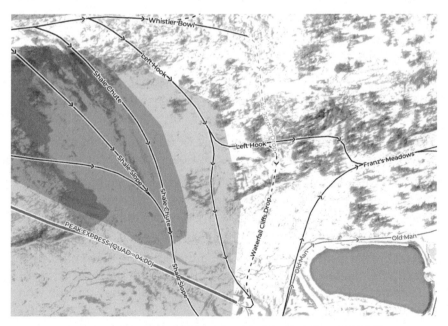

Air Jordan and the Waterfall Cliffs to the right of the Peak Express Chairlift.
(Source: Openskimap.org)

◆◆◆ Air Jordan: Air Jordan is a Triple-Black drop off a high cliff above Waterfall Cliffs. It has drops of 40 to 50 feet with only a small landing area below the cliff. It is accessible from East Ridge (Black), and then by continuing along the ridge above Left Hook (Black). This is a favorite of expert local freeride skiers and young rippers who like to drop down the front of the cliffs (to the enjoyment of those waiting in line at the Peak Express Chairlift base).

> **NOTE:** This is Triple-Black, expert territory with a massive drop and a difficult, small landing area that immediately leads to Waterfall Ridge.

◆◆◆ The Coffin: The Coffin is an extremely difficult, narrow Triple-Black chute just below the Peak Express Chairlift. It gets its name from how narrow it is (just about one body wide).

> **NOTE:** The Coffin does not have an official difficulty designation but should be considered a Triple-Black run. This is for experts only. Approach with extreme caution!

◆◆◆ Waterfall Cliffs: Waterfall Cliffs is a line of cliffs to the right of the Peak Express Chairlift base and is the smaller sibling of Air Jordan (Triple Black) above it. It is accessible via East Ridge (Black) followed by Left Hook (Black). Waterfall Ridge is another favorite of freeride skiers and young rippers who like to drop down the front of the cliffs.

> **NOTE:** This is definitely Triple-Black territory with 30 to 40-foot drops.

Heading up the Peak Express Chairlift through the mist towards the sun. (Source: Alexandra Diana)

WHISTLER MOUNTAIN

Peak to Creek Run

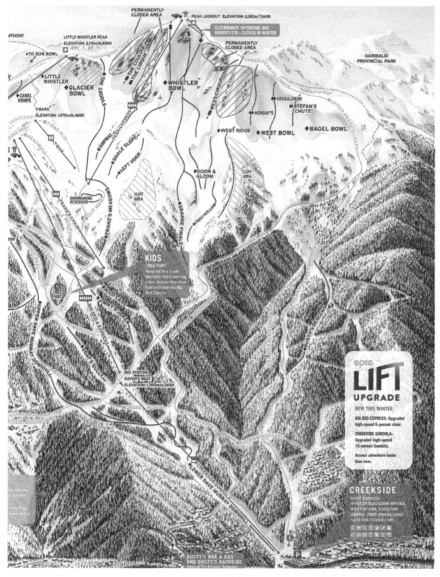

The Peak to Creek area of Whistler.
(Source: 2022/23 Whistler Blackcomb Trail Map)

*T*he Peak to Creek Area runs from Whistler Peak down Whistler Creekside. The main run—Peak to Creek—is one of the longest ski runs in North America at 11 kilometers with a 5,010-foot or 1,527-meter drop in elevation. If you want to test your stamina, this is a real 'leg burner' from top to bottom. When it is freshly groomed or covered in fresh snow, Peak to Creek is a wonderful long run.

This area also includes some challenging, 'abandoned' (never groomed, poorly maintained) Black runs off the left side of Peak to Creek (looking downhill). Only go exploring here if you are comfortable with challenging, off-piste skiing.

This area is definitely for strong intermediate and expert skiers and snowboarders.

Locals' Tips

- Whistler Blackcomb only occasionally grooms the Peak to Creek run, so check the Whistler Blackcomb website or Epic Mix app for its status. It if is groomed, locals will take advantage of this and run the Peak to Creek!

Gondolas/Lifts

Peak to Creek does not have its own gondola or lift. To access Peak to Creek, you need to take Creekside Gondola up, then the Big Red Express Chairlift, and then the Peak Express Chairlift. Peak to Creek starts at the top of the Peak Express Chairlift.

Lodges/Huts

There are no lodges or huts specifically associated with the Peak to Creek run. However, many people who make the Peak to Creek run reward themselves with food and/or drinks at Dusty's Bar and Grill at Creekside base.

Main Routes

There is no main Green route down the Peak to Creek area.

■ **Upper Peak to Creek – Lower Peak to Creek:** Upper and Lower Peak to Creek run from the top of the Peak Express Chairlift down to the Creekside base.

NOTE: If you see signs at the top of Lower Peak to Creek that read 'Experts Only', it means that the lower section of the run has not been groomed. If this sounds too challenging, you can follow Highway 86 down to the bottom of the Big Red Express Chairlift.

There is no main Black route down the Peak to Creek area.

Blue Runs

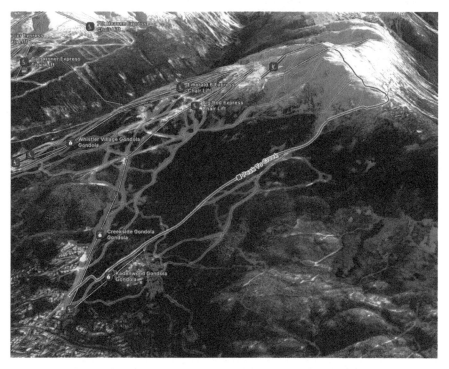

Peak to Creek running down from Whistler Peak to the Creekside base.
(Source: FATMAP.com)

■ **(Lower) Kadenwood Trail:** Lower Kadenwood Trail is a long, narrow, connector Blue run that starts on the left side (looking downhill) of Lower Dave Murray Downhill (Black), crosses Lower Franz's (Blue) and Lower Peak to Creek (Blue), and runs over to the Kadenwood neighborhood.

■ **(Upper) Kadenwood Trail:** Similar to Lower Kadenwood Trail (Blue), Upper Kadenwood Trail is a narrow, connector Blue run that starts on the left side (looking downhill) of Lower Kadenwood Trail

(Blue), crosses Lower Peak (Blue), and runs over to the Kadenwood neighborhood.

■ **(Upper) Peak to Creek:** Upper Peak to Creek is a steep, wide Blue run that starts at the top of the Peak Express Chairlift and runs through the open alpine zone at the top of Whistler Mountain. Upper Peak to Creek ends at the top of Lower Peak to Creek (Blue/Black) and Highway 86 (Blue).

NOTE: Normally groomed, this run can become quite bumpy and icy in spots due to heavy use.

■ **(Lower) Peak to Creek:** Lower Peak to Creek is very long Blue run that starts at the end of Upper Peak to Creek (Blue). At the end of Upper Peak to Creek, there is a fork in the run. Going right takes you down Highway 86 towards the Big Red Express Chairlift base. Going left takes you down Lower Peak to Creek to the Creekside base. This lower section has a variety of flatter and steeper sections, with options for some glade skiing on the left side of the run. The right side is a 'do not enter' creek zone.

NOTE: Whistler Blackcomb does not groom Peak to Creek very often anymore. If it is ungroomed, keep in mind that Lower Peak to Creek can be more like a Black run with moguls, ice, and other challenging terrain.

Black Runs/Areas

♦ **Big Timber:** Big Timber is a long, bumpy, ungroomed Black run to the left of Dusty's Descent (Black). It starts on Dusty's Descent and joins up with Lower Peak to Creek (Blue) above the Creekside base.

NOTE: Big Timber is not well maintained and has lots of trees, bumps, logs, and creek features, making it a challenging off-piste run.

♦ **Dusty's Descent:** Dusty's Descent is a bumpy, ungroomed Black run that starts and ends on Lower Peak to Creek (Blue).

NOTE: Dusty's Descent is not well maintained and has lots of trees, bumps, logs, and creek features, making it a challenging off-piste run.

♦ **Home Run:** Home Run is a narrow Black run from Big Timber into the Kadenwood neighborhood. This is definitely a zone for expert skier multi-millionaires—given the cost of the homes in the Kadenwood neighborhood!

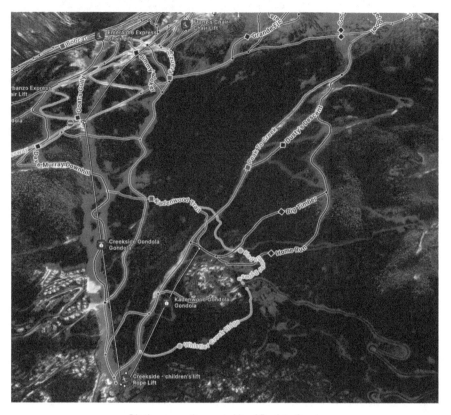

Black runs on the west side of Peak to Creek.
(Source: FATMAP.com)

Harmony Express Chairlift Area

The Harmony bowl area of Whistler. (Source: FATMAP.com)

The Harmony Express Chairlift area is one of the two large alpine bowl areas to the southeast of Whistler Peak (the other one being the Symphony Express Chairlift area). It is located between the Symphony Express Chairlift area to the east and Glacier Bowl/the Emerald Express Chairlift area to the west. Access to this area is mainly provided by the Harmony Express Chairlift, although you can also access part of it from the Glacier Bowl T-Bars.

This area has two main Blue runs, but it is better known for its Black runs and Double-Black chutes, drops, and faces. It is ideally suited for intermediate or expert skiers. On a day with fresh snow, this is where many locals head at the start of the day to look for fresh tracks.

NOTE: A lot of Harmony Bowl is in the alpine, so skiing can be difficult if visibility is poor. On a good snow day and most weekends, the bottom of the Harmony Express Chairlift can be very busy as both locals and visitors head to this area—so be prepared for a long wait in line.

Locals' Tips

- On a fresh snow/powder day, head down to the bottom of the Harmony Chairlift and get in line before it opens in order to get a chance at fresh tracks on the Harmony runs.
- The area below Pika's Traverse—for example Die Hard—offers great fresh tracks on a powder day.

Gondolas/Lifts

Harmony Express Chairlift: This is the high-speed, six-person chair that services the Harmony Bowl area.

Lodges/Huts

Harmony Base Shack: This is a small food shack offering drinks and basic food and snacks.

NOTE: This hut has not been open in recent years. It is unclear if it will open again.

Harmony Hut: This is a small hut at the top of the Harmony Express Chairlift. It offers warm drinks and some snacks but does not have an inside sitting area. There are washrooms in a small building behind the hut.

NOTE: Similar to the base shack, this hut has not been open in recent years. It is unclear if it will open again.

Main Routes

There is no main Green run from the top of the Harmony Express Chairlift to the chairlift base. Pika's Traverse (Green) starts at the top of the Harmony Express Chairlift but then curves across the top of the Harmony area to exit towards the Roundhouse Lodge area.

■ **Harmony Ridge:** Harmony Ridge is one of the two main Blue routes in the Harmony Express Chairlift area. It runs from Pika's Traverse (Green) down along the top of Harmony Ridge on the right side (looking downhill) of Harmony Bowl and ends at the bottom of the Harmony Express Chairlift.

■ **Harmony Piste – GS Run:** This is the other main Blue route in Harmony Bowl. It starts about halfway down Pika's Traverse (Green) and then curves through Harmony Bowl, ending on Sidewinder (Green), which leads over to the bottom of the Emerald Express Chairlift. Near the bottom, you can turn right (looking downhill) and go down the steep lower part of GS Run (Blue) to the bottom of the Harmony Express Chairlift.

There is no main Black run from the top to the bottom of the Harmony Express Chairlift.

Green Runs

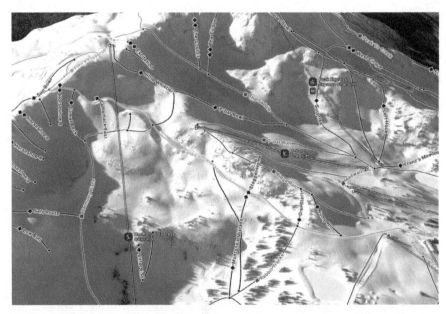

Pika's Traverse curving down from the top of the Harmony Express Chairlift, across the top of Harmony Bowl, and over to the Roundhouse Lodge area. (Source: FATMAP.com)

● **Burnt Stew Trail:** Burnt Stew Trail is a long Green run that starts at the top of the Harmony Express Chairlift, curves through

Symphony Bowl, and exits back into the Harmony Express Chairlift area where it ends on Harmony Ridge (Blue). The last third of the trail is very flat, so be prepared to do some skating and poling to get to the Harmony Ridge run.

> **NOTE**: Although this is a Green run, it does have a couple of steeper sections that can get quite bumpy with use. It should be considered a harder/darker Green. The last third of the trail is also very flat and can be very busy, as it is the only exit out of Symphony Bowl.

Heading down Burnt Stew Trail into Symphony Bowl on a bluebird day. (Source: Greg Chen)

● **Pika's Traverse:** Pika's Traverse is a long Green run from the top of the Harmony Express Chairlift over to the Roundhouse Lodge area. It starts as a medium-wide run, heads a short way down along Harmony Ridge, makes a very sharp left turn (looking downhill), narrows, and heads across and behind the Camel Backs (Black) and over towards the Roundhouse Lodge area.

> **NOTE**: The last two thirds of this run is quite narrow, and can be very busy, as it is the main exit from Harmony Bowl over to the Roundhouse Lodge area.

Blue Runs

■ **GS Run:** The GS Run is a Blue run from the top of the Emerald Express Chairlift down to the bottom of the Harmony Express Chairlift. This run has flatter and steeper sections with lots of ungroomed snow on either side. The first section from the top of the Emerald Express Chairlift is quite flat and even a bit uphill, so pick up some speed if you want to get across it.

> **NOTE**: The bottom of this run, below where it crosses Harmony Piste (Blue), is a wide, steep Blue that can get icy and bumpy from heavy traffic.

Heading down GS Run towards the bottom of the Harmony Express Chairlift.
(Source: Susan Rogers)

■ **Harmony Ridge:** Harmony Ridge is a long, groomed Blue run with some steep sections that starts on Pika's Traverse (Green) and ends at the Harmony Express Chairlift base. On a clear day, this run offers amazing views of Blackcomb Mountain and into the mountains of Garibaldi Provincial Park. Many consider it one of the most beautiful Blues on all of Whistler Blackcomb. From Harmony Ridge, you can drop into Harmony Bowl on the left side and Symphony Bowl on the right to access Black and Double-Black runs and chutes.

■ **Harmony Piste:** Harmony Piste is a Blue run that curves down through the middle of Harmony Bowl. This run is normally groomed but can get bumpy with heavy use or after a dump of fresh snow. It starts on the right of Pika's Traverse (Green) just past the Camel Backs (Black). Harmony Piste initially curves under the Camel Backs, providing access to the open alpine center of Harmony Bowl on the left side. It then curves downhill, swings left across the middle of Harmony Bowl, and ends down on Sidewinder (Green), which heads over to the bottom of the Emerald Express Chairlift.

The big Blue runs—Harmony Ridge, Harmony Piste, and the GS run—of the Harmony Express Chairlift area. (Source: FATMAP.com)

■ **Krummholtz:** Krummholtz is a short Blue run that connects Harmony Ridge (Blue) with Harmony Piste (Blue). It runs below Kaleidoscope (Black) and KC Roll (Double Black) and above and Boomer Bowl (Black) below. It is normally groomed but can get bumpy with use.

■ **Rabbit Tracks:** Rabbit Tracks is a short, ungroomed Blue run from below the end of Pika's Traverse (Green) down to GS Run (Blue). With fresh snow, this can be a wonderful spot for some lines through the pow.

NOTE: Watch out for 'snow snakes' (small trees) poking up through the snow that might catch your skis.

■ **Ridge Run:** Ridge Run is a narrow (very narrow in spots), ungroomed Blue run across the ridge from the top of the Glacier Bowl T-bar over to the top of the Emerald Express Chairlift. This run provides access to short Blue and Black/Double-Black runs on either side of the ridge.

> **NOTE:** The first part of Ridge Run is a bit uphill, so it will take some work to get up it.

■ **The Glades:** The Glades is an ungroomed, Blue alpine glade run on the right side (looking downhill) of Harmony Ridge. With fresh powder, this is a wonderful, open glade area to enjoy. It starts on the right side (looking downhill) of Harmony Ridge (Blue) and exits back onto it further down the hill.

> **NOTE:** Do not go too far to the right on this run or you may end up going down Harvey's (Black) or Robertson's (Black). Both are steep Black glade runs that lead down to Burnt Stew Trail (Green).

Black Runs/Areas

◆ **Big Daddy:** Big Daddy is an unmarked Black run that curves down from Harmony Piste (Blue) through the off-piste area in the middle of Harmony Bowl and ends up back on Harmony Piste further downhill. With fresh snow, this can be a fun off-piste skiing area. Big Daddy provides access to the top of Bitter End (Black) and Waterface (Black) next to the Harmony Waterfall Cliff.

◆ **Bitter End:** Bitter End is one of the two short, steep runs/drops on the left side (looking uphill) of Harmony Waterfall Ridge (Double Black). It runs below and to the right of the Harmony Express Chairlift.

> **NOTE:** The landing for this drop is onto a steep slope that is often bumpy.

◆ **Boot Chutes:** The Boot Chutes are two narrow, parallel Black chutes between the trees on the slope beside Lower McConkey's (Black). Access to Boot Chutes is from Harmony Piste (Blue) just past the entrance to Lower McConkey's.

Some of Harmony's lower Black runs, including the Gun Barrels, Boomer Bowl, and Lower McConkey's. (Source: FATMAP.com)

◆ **Boomer Bowl:** Boomer Bowl is a Black bowl on the left side (looking uphill) of Harmony Bowl. It is ungroomed and normally bumpy but can be quite fun with good/fresh snow. You can access it either from Harmony Ridge (Blue) or Krumholtz (Blue) that run above it. Exit this bowl by heading left over to Lower McConkey's (Black).

> **NOTE:** If you continue straight or exit towards the right from Boomer Bowl, you will enter Wet Dreams (Black), a difficult Black glade area.

◆ **Camel Backs:** The Camel Backs are two small hill features (a recessional moraine) underneath and to the left of the Harmony Express Chairlift. You can access different routes down the front of the Camel Backs from Pika's Traverse (Green) that runs behind this feature. The area below Camel Backs is a locals' favorite for steep first tracks in powder snow.

♦ **Gun Barrels:** The Gun Barrels are two narrow, steep Black chutes that run between the trees on the one side of Boomer Bowl (Black). These two chutes can be accessed from the left of Harmony Ridge (Blue) just past Boomer Bowl, and they exit down to the bottom of the Harmony Express Chairlift.

> **NOTE**: This is definitely an expert skiing zone and requires significant skill to successfully navigate the narrow, complex, tree-lined chutes.

Harmony Horseshoe Bowl's steep entrance chutes with 7th Heaven in the background across the valley. (Source: Nick Jones)

♦ **Horseshoe Bowl and Lower Horseshoe Bowl:** Horseshoe Bowl is the wide open, ungroomed, Black bowl area below Harmony Ridge. All the Harmony Horseshoe chutes end in this bowl area. Lower Horseshoe Bowl is the smaller, ungroomed, Black bowl area below the middle of Harmony Ridge.

> **NOTE**: The ski patrol regularly blasts the cornices along this side of Harmony Bowl. As a result, the slope below the cornices is often littered with cornice and avalanche debris, which can be rock-hard and should be avoided.

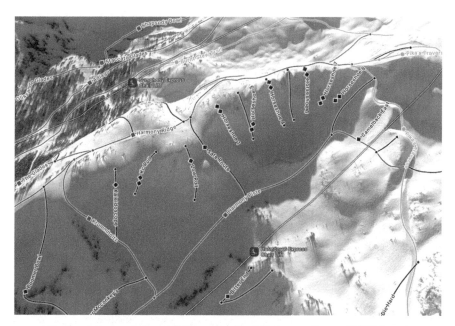

Harmony's famous (infamous?) Horseshoe Bowl Black runs. (Source: FATMAP.com)

◆◆ **Horseshoe Bowl Entrances (#1 and #3–8):** The Horseshoe Bowl Entrances are a series of challenging, Double-Black chute entrances into Harmony Horseshoe Bowl over the cornice that runs along the east wall of the bowl. Horseshoe #5 (H5) is considered to be the most difficult of these chutes with its steep, narrow, difficult entrance. There is no Horseshoe #2; instead, this run is called Upper McConkey's (Black). All the Horseshoe Bowl chute entrances are accessible from the left side of Harmony Ridge (Blue).

> **NOTE**: The slope below the cornices is often littered with cornice and avalanche debris, which can be rock-hard, so ski with caution.

◆ **Kaleidoscope:** Kaleidoscope is a short, ungroomed Black run into the area above Krummholz (Blue). Along with Low Roll (Black) and Safe Route (Black), this is one of the easier, single Black entrances into the Lower Horseshoe Bowl. You can access this run at the top from Harmony Ridge (Blue) and exit onto Krummholtz (Blue) below.

◆◆ **KC Roll:** KC Roll is a short, steep, bumpy Double-Black chute with a steep entrance between Kaleidoscope (Black) and Low Roll (Black). It is accessible from Harmony Ridge (Blue) at the top, and it exits onto Krummholtz (Blue) at the bottom.

◆◆ Little Whistler Bowl: Little Whistler Bowl is the small, steep, bumpy Black bowl below the top of the Harmony Express Chairlift and above Pika's Traverse (Green). You can access Little Whistler Bowl from below the top of the Harmony Express Chairlift and choose from a variety of lines down the front of this face. Little Whistler Bowl exits onto Pika's Traverse at the bottom. Sitting on the Harmony Express Chairlift, you can get a great view of people carving down the front of this bowl showing their 'stuff'.

MOUNTAIN NOTES

Harmony Horseshoe Bowl Cirque and Moraine

The Harmony Horseshoe Bowl is a nice example of a glacial cirque with a small recessional moraine in its lower end. A cirque is a bowl-shaped depression created by glacial erosion. Normally, a glacial cirque is open on the downhill side, and the cupped uphill section is usually quite steep. A recessional moraine is a ridge of debris across a valley or cirque that marks one of the endpoints of a glacier as it receded.

Sources: https://www.worldatlas.com/articles/mountain-and-glacial-landforms-what-is-a-cirque.html

https://www.worldatlas.com/articles/glacial-landforms-what-is-a-moraine.html

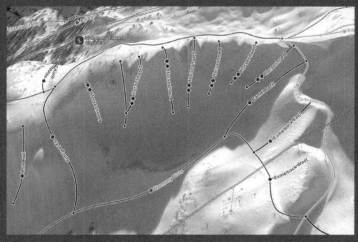

Horseshoe Bowl with its steep chutes.
(Source: FATMAP.com)

♦ **Low Roll:** Low Roll is one of the three easier Black entrances into the Lower Horseshoe Bowl. It sits between Safe Route (Black) and KC Role (Double Black). Low Roll and its neighboring runs are local favorites when there is fresh powder snow. You can access Low Roll from Harmony Ridge (Blue) and exit onto Harmony Piste (Blue) at the bottom.

♦ **(Upper) McConkey's:** Upper McConkey's is a steep, Black chute entrance into Harmony Horseshoe Bowl. It is accessible from Harmony Ridge (Blue) at the top and ends on Harmony Piste (Blue) below. Similar to the other Horseshoe Bowl chutes, the entrance is steep and narrow.

♦ **(Lower) McConkey's:** Lower McConkey's a wide, steep Black mogul run that starts at the top from Krummholtz (Blue) and runs down to the bottom of the Harmony Express Chairlift. Lower McConkey's is famous for its large, steep moguls.

♦ **Safe Route:** Safe Route is the easiest Black entrance from Harmony Ridge (Blue) into the Horseshoe Bowl below. You can access this run at the top from Harmony Ridge (Blue) and exit at the bottom onto Harmony Piste (Blue).

HISTORY NOTES

'Diamond' Jim McConkey

The McConkey's runs are named after Jim McConkey, the ski-school star of early Whistler Mountain. With a magnetic personality and an already distinguished ski career south of the border, Diamond Jim moved to Whistler in the spring of 1968 and invested all his money building a ski shop here. The risk proved wise, as new equipment and technology drew more people to the sport, which consequently created a greater market for instruction and gear. Jim managed the ski school until 1980 and the rental and retail operations until 1985.

Whistler Mountain honored Jim by naming Upper and Lower McConkey's runs after him on December 15, 1994—the same day that the Harmony Express Chairlift was opened. A true lover of fun with an infectious joy for mountain life, McConkey's catchphrase—Every day's a bonus—is one we can all learn from.

Source: https://www.whistler.com/blog/post/2015/02/27/whats-in-a-name-whistler-mountain-ski-runs/

♦ **Waterface:** Waterface is one of the two short, steep runs/drops on the left side (looking uphill) of Harmony Waterfall Ridge (Double Black). The landing from this drop is into a steep slope that is often bumpy. Coming up on the Harmony Express Chairlift, you can often see young rippers dropping down this cliff face.

Other Areas

♦ **Die Hard:** Die Hard is a steep, ungroomed Black area that spills over the smoother right end (looking uphill) of Harmony Waterfall Ridge (Double Black). It starts on the right side (looking downhill) of Pika's Traverse (Green), and then runs down to meet with the GS Run (Blue). This is a locals' favorite for steep, fresh powder lines and one of my personal favorite runs on a fresh snow day.

♦ **Die Hard Start:** Die Hard Start is a short, steep, bumpy Black face just below Ridge Run (Blue) and above Pika's Traverse (Green). You can access Die Hard Start at the top from Ridge Run and exit onto Pika's Traverse at the bottom. You can then continue across Pika's and enter the top of Die Hard (Black).

> **NOTE:** This run drops onto Pika's Traverse. Exercise caution and control when exiting this run to avoid hitting other skiers on the run below.

♦ **GS Start:** GS Start is a short, bumpy Black run just below Ridge Run (Blue) and above Pika's Traverse (Green). You can access this run at the top from Ridge Run and exit onto Pika's Traverse at the bottom. You can continue across Pika's to enter the top of Rabbit Tracks (Blue).

> **NOTE:** Similar to DH Start, this run drops onto Pika's Traverse, so be cautious at the bottom to avoid hitting skiers on the run below.

♦ **Jacob's Ladder:** Jacob's Ladder is a Black run that traverses across the top left (looking downhill) of Little Whistler Bowl (Black). It then runs down along Little Whistler Ridge towards the top of the T-Bars. Advanced intermediate and expert skiers use this route as a shortcut to get to Pika's Traverse (Green) or to Ridge Run (Blue) to head over to the Roundhouse Lodge. This run also gives you access to runs down into Glacier Bowl (Black).

◆ **Jump Hill:** Jump Hill is a short, bumpy Black run just below the end of Ridge Run (Blue) and above Pika's Traverse (Green). You can access it at the top from Ridge Run and exit onto Pika's Traverse at the bottom.

> **NOTE:** Use caution at the bottom, as there can be a sharp drop. Also exercise caution and control when exiting this run to avoid hitting other skiers.

◆◆ **Harmony Waterfall Ridge:** Harmony Waterfall Ridge is a large cliff face that runs across Harmony Bowl from the center of the bowl towards the Roundhouse Lodge area. It gets its name from the frozen waterfalls that you can see on the face of the cliff. Waterface (Black) runs down the left side (looking uphill) of the cliff and Die Hard (Black) runs down the right side. When you are on the Harmony Express Chairlift, watch for freeriders and rippers dropping down the front of this cliff.

> **NOTE**: This cliff face is 30 to 40 feet high in spots and should only be attempted by freeriders with the required expert skiing skills.

Harmony Waterfall Cliffs with Bitter End and Waterfall on the left and Die Hard on the right.
(Source: Nick Jones)

♦♦ **Staggerhome Chute:** Staggerhome Chute is a very steep, rocky Double-Black chute below Ridge Run (Blue) and above Pika's Traverse (Green).

> **NOTE**: Pika's Traverse is close to and directly below this chute. Exercise caution and control when exiting to avoid falling onto Pika's Traverse and hitting other skiers.

♦ **Harmony Chairlift Line:** This is an unmarked, ungroomed, bumpy Black 'run' with steep sections, drops, and trees. It starts at Harmony Piste (Blue) and runs under the Harmony Express Chairlift. The lift is very close to this run in some spots, providing a great view of skiers going down it.

> **NOTE:** The access path to the top of this run is a bit uphill, so it takes some work to reach it before going downhill.

♦♦ **Wet Dreams:** Wet Dreams is a challenging, ungroomed Double-Black glade area at the bottom and right of Boomer Bowl (Black). You can access this area from the bottom of Boomer Bowl, and the exit at the bottom is onto the end of the Gun Barrels (Black). This is a favorite of expert locals looking for challenging powder runs in between trees.

> **NOTE**: This area can have large bumps, tight turns, and steep faces. When entering this area, stay left, as there is a steep, un-skiable cliff on the right side.

Lower McConkey's famous moguls with Boot Chutes on the right, seen from the bottom of the Harmony Express Chairlift. (Source: Nick Jones).

Symphony Express Chairlift Area

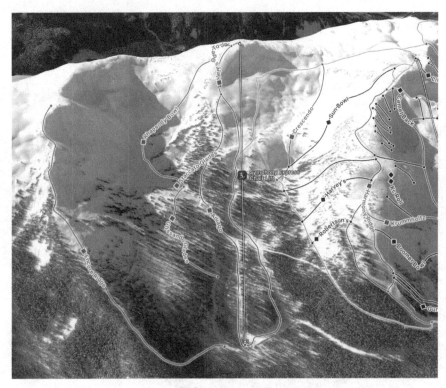

The Symphony Bowl area of Whistler. (Source: FATMAP.com)

The Symphony Express Chairlift Area is the furthest southeast ski area on Whistler. It includes the wonderful large open alpine Symphony Bowl with lots of Blue and Black runs and glade-skiing options as well as access to the Flute Bowls area.

The main access route into the Symphony area is down Burnt Stew Trail (Green) from the top of the Harmony Express Chairlift. Burnt Stew curves down into Symphony and then exits back towards the Harmony Express Chairlift area again. You can follow Burnt Stew into Symphony Bowl and then branch off onto runs leading into the glades at the bottom of this area such as Jeff's Ode-to-Joy (Blue) and Adagio (Blue). Sun Bowl (Black) is another fun route into Symphony when there is good visibility and snow. You can access Sun Bowl from Harmony Ridge (Blue).

This area is ideally suited for intermediate and expert skiers. Advanced beginners can also ski through this area by sticking to Burnt Stew Trail (Green).

> **NOTE:** Much of Symphony Bowl is in the alpine, so this area can be difficult to ski if visibility is poor. The bottom of Symphony can also get very, very busy on a good snow day and most weekends due to the popularity of this area.

Locals' Tips

- On a fresh snow/powder day, take the Harmony Express Chairlift up to the top and continue directly down Burnt Stew Trail (Green) into Symphony even before the Symphony Express Chairlift opens. You can get fresh tracks in powder on either side of Burnt Stew Trail and down Crescendo (Blue). Remember to stay on Burnt Stew Trail to get back to the Harmony Express Chairlift base, otherwise you may get stuck at the bottom of the Symphony Chairlift before it opens.
- Similar to going down Burnt Stew Trail into Symphony Bowl, on a fresh snow/powder day you can access Sun Bowl (Black) from the right side (looking downhill) of Harmony Ridge (Blue) for fresh tracks. If the Symphony Express Chairlift is not open yet, remember to exit via Burnt Stew Trail.

Gondolas/Lifts

Symphony Express Chairlift: This is the high-speed, four-person chairlift that services Symphony Bowl area.

Lodges/Huts

There are no lodges or huts in Symphony Bowl. However, there are washrooms at the bottom of Symphony Express Chairlift.

Main Routes

● **Burnt Stew Trail:** Burnt Stew Trail is the only Green run in Symphony Bowl. It starts at the top of the Harmony Express Chairlift, curves down into Symphony, and then exits back towards the Harmony Express Chairlift area.

> **NOTE:** There is no Green run from the top of the Symphony Express Chairlift down to the bottom of the chairlift.

■ **Jeff's Ode to Joy:** Jeff's Ode to Joy is the main Blue run from the top of the Symphony Express Chairlift down through Symphony Bowl, through the glades, and ends at the bottom of the chairlift. If you want to exit the Symphony area, remember to turn left onto Burnt Stew Trail (Green) towards the Harmony Express Chairlift area.

There is no full Black route from the top of Symphony Bowl down to the bottom of the Symphony Express Chairlift.

Green Runs

● **Burnt Stew Trail:** Burnt Stew Trail is a Green run that starts at the top of the Harmony Express Chairlift, curves down into Symphony Bowl, and then exits towards the Harmony Express Chairlift area. This trail is quite narrow in spots and has a couple of steep spots that can get skied out and bumpy towards the end of day. It is definitely a harder Green run.

> **NOTE:** Burnt Stew Trail is the only exit out of Symphony Bowl. To exit Symphony, ski halfway down and then follow Burnt Stew Trail out and over to the bottom of the Harmony Express Chairlift.

Blue Runs

■ **Adagio:** Adagio is a Blue run that forks off to the right (looking downhill) from Jeff's Ode to Joy (Blue) and runs down through the trees to the bottom of the Harmony Express Chairlift. The top section near the tree line has steep sections that can get quite bumpy with use. The lower section is normally a wide, groomed run that goes down to the bottom of the Symphony Express Chairlift.

■ **Glissando Glades:** The Glissando Glades is an area of relatively flat Blue glades at the bottom of Rhapsody Bowl (Blue). There is normally a narrow, groomed path through this area leading down to the bottom of the Symphony Express Chairlift. There are opportunities on either side for glade skiing, but be aware that the slope is very shallow in this area.

> **NOTE**: There is a creek that runs down the right side (looking downhill) of this area. Look for and obey all warning signs to avoid getting stuck in a creek hole.

Blue runs in the top half of the Symphony area including Rhapsody Bowl, Jeff's Ode to Joy, Adagio, and Crescendo. (Source: FATMAP.com)

HISTORY NOTES

Burnt Stew Trail

In the summer of 1958, before Whistler Mountain became a ski hill, Florence Petersen, Kelly Fairhurst, and Don Gow were on a backpacking trip around the mountain. After setting up camp one evening, they started cooking some stew for dinner in an old billy can over a fire. As the story goes, nobody remembered to stir the pot, resulting in the stew getting burnt and giving this run its name.

Source: https://www.whistler.com/blog/post/2015/02/27/whats-in-a-name-whistler-mountain-ski-runs/

Symphony Bowl with fresh snow, looking up at Piccolo Peak. (Source: Elena Generalova)

■ **Jeff's Ode to Joy:** Jeff's Ode to Joy is the big, groomed Blue run from the top of the Symphony Express Chairlift down through Harmony Bowl to the bottom of the chairlift. This run has a couple of quite steep sections and can get bumpy as it gets skied out during the day. There are also a couple of dips and humps, so watch out for these and maintain your speed so that you don't get stuck. Jeff's Ode to Joy provides access to ungroomed alpine areas on either side that offer amazing powder skiing on a fresh snow day. Remember that if you want to exit the Symphony Bowl area, look for the signs and turn left (looking downhill) onto Burnt Stew Trail (Green), which will take you out and over to the bottom of the Harmony Express Chairlift.

■ **Rhapsody Bowl:** Rhapsody Bowl a big, ungroomed Blue alpine bowl below Flute Summit. This bowl is wonderful for powder lines when there is fresh snow. You can access this area by skiing to the right from Jeff's Ode to Joy (Blue) just below the top of the Symphony Express Chairlift. Rhapsody Bowl ends in the Glissando Glades (Blue) area, which leads down to the bottom of the Symphony Express Chairlift.

■ **Sierra:** Sierra is similar to Crescendo (Blue) and is an ungroomed Blue route below Burnt Stew Trail (Green). It starts on the right side (looking downhill) of Burnt Stew Trail below the Piccolo Summit and curves down through Symphony Bowl to end on Crescendo.

■ **Staccato Glades:** The Staccato Glades is a short area of Blue glades accessible from the right side (looking downhill) of Adagio (Blue). These glades end into the Rhapsody Bowl (Blue) and Glissando Glades (Blue).

HISTORY NOTES

Whistler's Musical Theme

In the 1960s, the Garibaldi Lift Company started to develop Whistler as a ski destination. The company's founder, Franz Wilhelmsen, was a Norwegian who had a passion for both skiing and music. Rumor has it that to create a unique and memorable identity for the resort, he decided to incorporate musical names into the mountain's features. Apparently, this was inspired by his love for classical music. As a result, many of the mountain features at Whistler Blackcomb were named after musical terms or instruments, such as Harmony Bowl, Symphony Bowl, and Piccolo Summit. The tradition has been continued as the resort expanded over the years, and the musical theme has become an integral part of Whistler's identity.

Flute Summit, Symphony Bowl, Piccolo Summit, Harmony Ridge, and Black Tusk in the background. Seen from the top of 7th Heaven. (Source: Nick Jones)

Looking up at the Flute Summit from Rhapsody Bowl.
(Source: Elena Generalova)

Black Runs/Areas

Harmony Ridge

Harmony Ridge is the ridge that runs between the Harmony and Symphony Bowls. Harmony Ridge (Blue) runs down this ridge providing access to the Black and Double-Black runs on either side.

♦ **Harvey's:** Harvey's is one of the routes into Symphony Bowl from Harmony Ridge (Blue). It is a steep, bumpy Black at the top with glades at the bottom. This run exits onto Burnt Stew Trail (Green) at the bottom, where you can either take Burnt Stew Trail out to the bottom of the Harmony Express Chairlift or you can cross Burnt Stew Trail and continue through the glades below down to Jeff's Ode to Joy (Blue).

> **NOTE**: The lower slope of Harvey's is quite steep directly above Burnt Stew Trail. It is important to exercise control so that you don't ski (or fall) onto Burnt Stew Trail too quickly, as it can be very busy with traffic exiting out of the Symphony area.

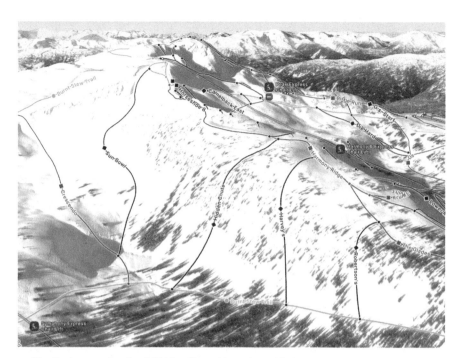

The Black runs—Sun Bowl, Hidden Chute, Harvey's, and Robertson's—that come down from Harmony Ridge into the Symphony Bowl area. (Source: FATMAP.com)

◆ **Hidden Chute:** Hidden Chute is another route into Symphony Bowl from Harmony Ridge (Blue). As the name suggests, the entrance is not easily visible from Harmony Ridge—you need to ski across a flat section to the right of Harmony Ridge to see the top of the chute. This Black chute is steep at the top, with steep glades at the bottom. It exits onto Burnt Stew Trail (Green), which leads back to the Harmony Express Chairlift base area. You can also cross Burnt Stew Trail and continue through the glades below down to Jeff's Ode to Joy (Blue).

> **NOTE**: Similar to Harvey's, the lower slope of this run is quite steep directly above Burnt Stew Trail. Exercise control so that you don't ski (or fall) onto Burnt Stew Trail too quickly.

◆ **Robertson's:** Robertson's is the third route into Symphony Bowl from Harmony Ridge (Blue). This Black chute is steep and bumpy at the top, with old-growth tree glades at the bottom. It exits at the bottom onto Burnt Stew Trail (Green), which leads back to the bottom of the Harmony Express Chairlift. You can also cross Burnt

Stew Trail and continue through the glades below down to Jeff's Ode to Joy (Blue).

> **NOTE**: Similar to Harvey's and Hidden Chute, the lower slope of this run is quite steep directly above Burnt Stew Trail. Exercise control so that you don't ski (or fall) onto Burnt Stew Trail too quickly.

◆ **Sun Bowl:** Sun Bowl is one of my favorite Black runs on Whistler. It is a wonderful, bumpy Black bowl that leads down into the Symphony Bowl area. You can access Sun Bowl at the top from Pika's Traverse (Green). The bottom of Sun Bowl ends in the large, flat bottom of Symphony Bowl, from where you can either exit towards the left down a steep mogul face to Burnt Stew Trail (Green) or continue towards the right for an easier route to Burnt Stew Trail. Sun Bowl faces southeast, so it gets lots of sunshine in the morning, and as a result, it is one of the first faces to soften on a cold day.

> **NOTE**: Because Sun Bowl faces southeast and gets a lot of sun, it is also prone to thaw/freeze cycles, which can make it very hard/icy and challenging to ski.

Sun Bowl and Sun Bowl Chutes seen from the side of Harmony Ridge on a bluebird day.
(Source: Elena Generalova)

♦ **Sun Bowl Chutes:** The Sun Bowl Chutes are a couple of steep, narrow Black chutes in the cliff face to the right of Sun Bowl (Black). Access these chutes by traversing to the right of the top of Sun Bowl's entrance from Pika's Traverse (Green). These chutes exit onto the bottom of Sun Bowl.

> **NOTE:** These chutes are narrow and an expert skier zone. Approach with caution!

Piccolo Summit

The Piccolo Summit is the peak above Symphony Bowl and next to the top of the Symphony Express Chairlift. It has several Black and Double-Black runs that come down its frontside.

♦ **Piccolo Main:** Piccolo Main is a steep, bumpy Black face that is the easier of the three routes down the front of Piccolo Summit. You can access this face by going right at the top of the Symphony Express Chairlift and traversing across in front of and past Piccolo Summit. This run ends down on Burnt Stew Trail (Green).

♦♦ **Piccolo North Face:** Piccolo North Face is a very difficult, steep, bumpy Double-Black face directly below the top of the Symphony Express Chairlift. You can access this run by going right and down behind the top of the Symphony Express Chairlift.

> **NOTE:** This is a very steep face that can get bare and icy, requiring expert skills to negotiate.

♦♦ **Piccolo Summit Slope:** Similar to Piccolo North Face (Double Black), this is a very steep, bumpy Double-Black face below Piccolo Summit. Access this run by going right at the top of the Symphony Express Chairlift and then traversing over to under the summit.

> **NOTE:** This is a very steep face that can get bare and icy, requiring expert skills to negotiate. Approach with caution.

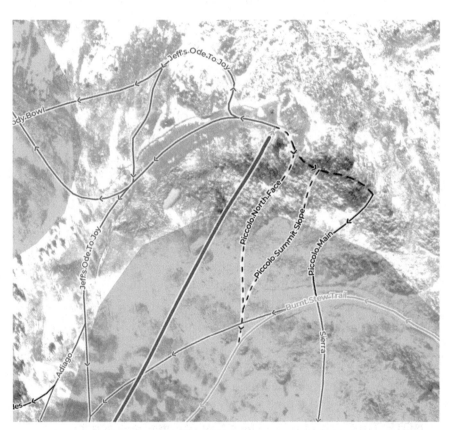

The Black runs coming down from the front of Piccolo Summit including Piccolo North Face, Piccolo Summit Slope, and Piccolo Main. (Source: Openskimap.org)

Alex Jones Cree ripping down Sun Bowl Chute.
(Source: Owen Jones Cree)

Flute Bowl Area

The Flute Bowl area of Whistler.
(Source: FATMAP.com)

The Flute Bowl area is a large, off-piste area to the southeast of the Symphony Express Chairlift area. This area provides amazing side-country skiing opportunities that are still within the boundaries of the Whistler Blackcomb Resort.

Access to the Flute Bowl area is via the Symphony Express Chairlift. From the top of the chairlift, you can ski over to the side of the Flute Bowl area and then hike or 'skin up' to Flute Summit and Encore Ridge. To get to the path up to the summit, ski to the right from Jeff's Ode to Joy (Blue) in the direction of Rhapsody Bowl (Blue). Instead of turning left down to Rhapsody Bowl, continue to the base of the uphill path, which is clearly visible on the right slope (looking uphill) of Flute Summit. The boot hike up this path takes about 15 minutes.

Although the Flute Bowl is still within the resort boundaries and is patrolled by the Whistler Blackcomb Ski Patrol, this is an expert level, near-backcountry skiing zone.

NOTES:

- If visibility is poor and you cannot clearly see the uphill path from Jeff's Ode to Joy, save the Flute Bowl for another day. The entire area is open alpine with little to no defining features, making it extremely challenging when visibility is poor.
- The cornices around the edge of Flute Bowl are large and potentially dangerous. Approach with caution and look for routes already skied by others.
- The area below the cornice is often littered with avalanche debris from Whistler Blackcomb Ski Patrol blasting, so ski with caution.

The Flute Bowl area as seen from the top of the Symphony Express Chairlift.
(Source: Nick Jones)

Gondolas/Lifts

Symphony Express Chairlift: This is the high-speed, four-person chairlift that you need to take to access the Flute Bowl area.

If you have touring skis and skins, you can also 'skin' from Burnt Stew Trail (Green) up and over towards the Flute Bowl area.

Lodges/Huts

There are no lodges or huts in the Flute Bowl, but there are washrooms at the bottom of the Symphony Express Chairlift.

Main Routes

◆◆ **Flute Main Bowl:** The Flute Main Bowl is the first of the three Flute Bowls. It is a Double-Black area with steep entrances over a cornice and exits down into Rhapsody Bowl (Blue).

All of the Flute Bowl runs/routes are equally challenging and present viable routes down into Rhapsody Bowl.

Green and Blue Runs

There are no Green or Blue runs in the Flute Bowl area.

Black Runs/Areas

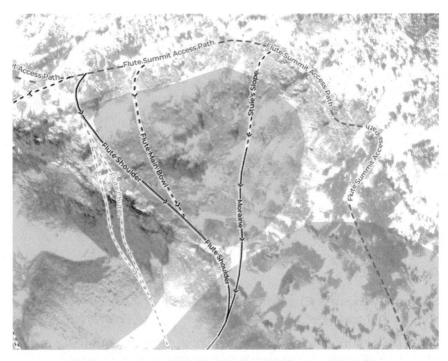

Main Flute Bowl showing Flute Shoulder, Flute Main Bowl, and Stuie's Slope.
(Source: Openskimap.org)

◆◆ **Big O:** The Big O is a Double-Black route that runs across the ridge between North Flute Bowl and Lesser Flute Bowl. At the end of the ridge, you can either go left (looking downhill) into the North Flute Bowl or right into Lesser Flute Bowl. Both routes exit down into Rhapsody Bowl (Blue).

> **NOTE**: Both of these routes down from the ridge are very steep and require expert skiing skills.

◆ **Encore Ridge:** Encore Ridge is a long Black run that curves back down from Flute Summit to the bottom of the Symphony Express Chairlift. It follows the ski area boundary and provides access to the Flute Bowl entrances on the left side of the run.

Stuie's Slope and Flute Main Bowl seen from Flute Shoulder. (Source: Abel Tan)

◆◆◆ **Flute Chutes:** The Flute Chutes are a pair of Triple-Black chutes that are considered the hardest entrance into any of the Flute Bowls. Access to these chutes is over a cornice into very steep, rocky chutes that exit down into Rhapsody Bowl (Blue).

> **NOTE**: Do not attempt these chutes without some guidance from someone who has experience skiing them.

◆◆ **Flute Main Bowl:** The Flute Main Bowl is the first of the three Flute Bowls. It is a Double-Black area with steep entrances over a cornice and exits down into Rhapsody Bowl (Blue).

♦♦ Flute North Bowl: The Flute North Bowl is the second and largest Flute Bowl area below the Flute Summit. This is a Double-Black area with steep entrances over the cornice and exits down into Rhapsody Bowl (Blue).

♦♦ Flute Shoulder: Flute Shoulder is a Double-Black route between Flute Main Bowl and Flute North Bowl. It starts with an easy roll entrance followed by an increasingly steep slope that exits into Rhapsody Bowl (Blue) below.

Lesser and North Flute Bowls including Flute Chutes, Flute North Bowl, North Bowl Cornice, Big O, and Lesser Flute Bowl. (Source: Openskimap.org)

♦ Lesser Flute Bowl: Lesser Flute Bowl is the smallest bowl of the three Flute Bowls. This is also the last bowl area accessible from Encore Ridge (Black) before it descends into the tree line and exits out towards the bottom of the Symphony Express Chairlift. Most people don't venture this far down Encore Ridge (dropping instead into Flute Main Bowl or Flute North Bowl), and as a result, it can offer pockets of untracked snow.

♦ Moraine: The Moraine is a Black route that runs down the front of the moraine that is located in the bottom middle of Main Flute Bowl. It exits down into Rhapsody Bowl (Blue).

◆◆ North Bowl Cornice: The North Bowl Cornice is the Double-Black entrance into North Flute Bowl that is furthest down Encore Ridge (Blue). This route starts with a steep entrance over the cornice and exits down into Rhapsody Bowl (Blue).

◆◆ Stuie's Slope: Stuie's Slope is the first Double-Black entrance into Main Flute Bowl at the top of the Flute Summit access route. This route starts with a steep entrance over the cornice and exits down onto the moraine in the bottom middle of Main Flute Bowl.

Lesser Flute on the left and North Flute Bowl on the right. Big O runs down the ridge between the two bowls, and Flute Chutes can be seen on the upper right. (Source: Michael Rivera)

PEAK 2 PEAK GONDOLA

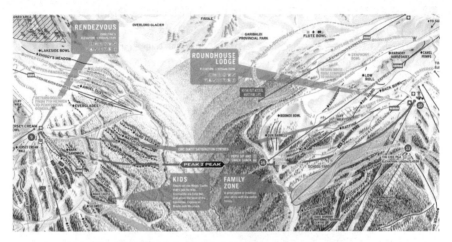

The Peak 2 Peak Gondola between Whistler and Blackcomb.
(Source: 2022/23 Whistler Blackcomb Trail Map)

Opened in December 2008, the Peak 2 Peak Gondola is an iconic feature of the Whistler Blackcomb Ski Resort and is recognized for its amazing engineering. Connecting the alpine terrain of Whistler and Blackcomb Mountains, this remarkable gondola spans 4.4 kilometers (2.73 miles) in length and reaches an impressive height of 436 meters (1,430 feet) above the valley floor. As the longest and highest unsupported lift of its kind, the Peak 2 Peak Gondola offers riders unparalleled views of the stunning Coast Mountains and the Whistler Blackcomb Resort.

The Peak 2 Peak Gondola allows skiers and snowboarders to easily switch between Whistler and Blackcomb mountains at the alpine level in under 15 minutes. The gondola maximizes time spent on the slopes by reducing the time previously needed to travel down to the village base and then take chairlifts or gondolas up again.

Access to the Peak 2 Peak Gondola on Whistler Mountain is next to the Roundhouse Lodge. Access to the gondola on Blackcomb Mountain is next to the Rendezvous Lodge.

For a special treat, wait for one of the two gray gondolas with glass bottoms in order to get an amazing view directly below the gondola!

Looking towards Whistler Mountain from inside the Peak 2 Peak Gondola.
(Source: Greg Chen)

Blackcomb Mountain.
(Source: 2022/23 Whistler Blackcomb Trail Map)

Blackcomb Mountain is the other half of the Whistler Blackcomb Resort. Blackcomb opened as its own resort in 1980, competed with Whistler for 17 years, and then merged with Whistler in 1997 to create what we know today as Whistler Blackcomb.

Blackcomb Mountain gets its name from the distinctive black ridge at its summit. Early mountaineers and skiers thought that it looked like the comb of a rooster, hence the name.

The 'black comb' of Blackcomb Mountain seen on a bluebird spring day. (Source: Nick Jones)

Blackcomb has its own character and features, including a mix of challenging, steep terrain, open alpine bowls, wide groomers, mogul runs, and tree-lined runs. Blackcomb Mountain includes a total of 3,414 acres/13.8 square kilometers of skiable terrain, 16 lifts, and 100+ marked runs. The vertical drop is 5,280 feet/1,609 meters from the top of 7th Heaven down to the Blackcomb base (the greatest vertical drop in the combined resort area).

Similar to Whistler, Blackcomb can be divided into several areas including:

- Blackcomb Lower Frontside (Blackcomb Gondola and Excalibur Gondola)
- Blackcomb Upper Frontside (Blackcomb Gondola and Excelerator Express Chairlift)
- Catskinner Express Chairlift/Terrain Park Area
- Jersey Cream Express Chairlift

- Crystal Ridge Express Chairlift
- Glacier Express Chairlift
- Gemstone Bowls Area
- Blackcomb Glacier Area
- 7th Heaven Express Chairlift
- Saudan Couloir Area

BLACKCOMB MOUNTAIN

Lower Frontside Area

The Lower Frontside of Blackcomb.
(Source: 2022/23 Whistler Blackcomb Trail Map)

The Blackcomb Lower Frontside area is located on the lower part of Blackcomb above the Blackcomb base and below the Blackcomb Gondola Mid Station.

This area offers a range of Green and Blue runs and even some unmarked quasi-Black runs. Green Line is the main Green run that zigzags down the lower front side. Lower Gear Jammer, Upper Mainline, and Lower Cruiser are all good Blue runs. Generally, this area is well suited for beginner and intermediate skiers.

The Blackcomb Gondola is the way to upload onto Blackcomb from the Blackcomb base. You can either get off at the gondola mid station and ski the Lower Frontside, or you can take it to the top to Rendezvous Lodge.

Excalibur Gondola is the way to upload onto Blackcomb from the Whistler Village base. At the top of Excalibur, you can choose to either ski the Lower Frontside or take the Excelerator Express Chairlift further up the mountain.

Merlin's Pub is a classic ski pub at the Blackcomb base and a great spot for après ski. There are also other restaurants and coffee shops at the Blackcomb base/upper village.

Locals' Tips

- Being lower on the mountain, this area is a good option to consider if the weather/visibility is poor higher up in the alpine zone.
- On a warm spring day, skiing down to the Blackcomb base and having lunch at Merlin's Pub on their outdoor patio can be a wonderful midday break.
- In the spring, if conditions are very slushy and not your preferred type of skiing, you can always download on the Blackcomb Gondola or via the Excalibur Gondola.
- If you are staying somewhere in the Blackcomb Upper Benchlands, ask your host if it is possible to use the ski-out trails through the forest on the right side (looking downhill) of Lower Cruiser. This way you can ski out to your accommodation versus going to the Blackcomb base and taking the bus to get back home.

Gondolas/Lifts

Blackcomb Gondola: This is the new eight-person gondola that runs from the Blackcomb base area up to Rendezvous Lodge. The gondola slows down to allow entry/exit about halfway up the front side of Blackcomb at the Blackcomb Gondola Mid Station.

Excalibur Gondola: This is the eight-person gondola that runs from the Whistler base halfway up the front side of Blackcomb. The gondola slows down to allow entry/exit one third of the way up at the Excalibur Gondola Mid Station. People who park in Blackcomb Parking Lots 6, 7, and 8 use the mid station as their starting point to upload onto the mountain.

Magic Chairlift: This is the short, slow chairlift that runs from the Blackcomb base up to the Excalibur Gondola Mid Station area. It is primarily used by the ski school to get kids and beginners to the top of Yellow Brick Road (Green) for lessons. Magic Chairlift is one of the oldest chairs in Whistler Blackcomb and is a reminder of what chairlifts used to be like.

Lodges/Huts

Blackcomb Day Lodge: The Blackcomb Day Lodge is the main Whistler Blackcomb Resort building at the base of Blackcomb Mountain. It includes a customer service center, ticket booths, Merlin's Pub, Merlin's Cafe, a small shop (for clothing, gloves, goggles, etc.), washrooms, and a tuning and rental shop in the basement.

Main Routes

Green Line: This is the main Green run that zigzags across Blackcomb Lower Frontside. This lower section of Green Line starts just above the Blackcomb Gondola Mid Station, passes by the top of the Excalibur Gondola, and ends at the Blackcomb base area near the bottom of the Blackcomb Gondola.

Lower Cruiser: This is the main Blue run down the Blackcomb Lower Frontside. Lower Cruiser starts at the top of the Excalibur Gondola and runs down to end on Greenline (Green) just above the Blackcomb base area.

There are no Black routes from the top to the bottom of this area.

Green Runs

Green Line: Green Line is the main Green run that goes back and forth across the Blackcomb Lower Frontside. The lower section of Green Line starts just above the Blackcomb Gondola Mid Station, passes by the top of the Excalibur Gondola, and ends at the Blackcomb base area.

NOTE: This is the main route to the Blackcomb base. As a result, it can get quite busy and sometimes can get skied out due to traffic. In the spring, this lower section can be very slushy as well.

● **Village Run:** Village Run is a flat Green run that starts on the left side (looking downhill) of Green Line (Green) and runs past the Excalibur Gondola Mid Station area down to the Whistler Village base area. It is the only route that allows skiers on Blackcomb to cross over the roads and creek between the two mountains and get to Whistler Village. At the end of the day, it can get icy and/or slushy depending on the conditions.

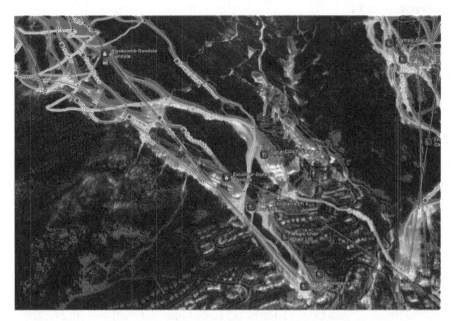

The Green Line running down the Blackcomb Lower Frontside to the Blackcomb base area. (Source: FATMAP.com)

● **Yellow Brick Road:** Yellow Brick Road is a short, easy Green run from the top of the Magic Chairlift back down to the Blackcomb base area.

NOTE: This run is used by the ski school for beginner ski lessons and can be quite busy with slow skiers.

Blue Runs

■ **Lower Cruiser:** Lower Cruiser is a wide, relatively easy Blue run that starts near the top of the Excalibur Gondola. It runs down to end on Green Line (Green) just above the Blackcomb base. It has both flat and steeper sections.

NOTE: Normally groomed, Lower Cruiser can get bumpy, icy, and/or slushy depending on the traffic and conditions. It is also one of the main ski-out routes to the Blackcomb base area, so it can get busy at the end of the day.

■ **Lower Gear Jammer:** Lower Gear Jammer is a Blue run with steep sections that starts from Easy Out (Green) on the Blackcomb Upper Frontside and ends down on Green Line (Green) just above the Blackcomb Tube Park. Not many people ski this run, so you can sometimes find untouched corduroy here later in the day.

NOTE: Lower Gear Jammer is often in the shade, so it can be quite hard/icy if it is cold.

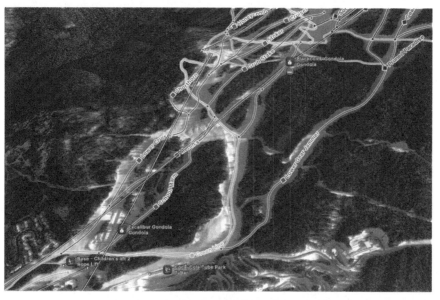

The main Blue runs in the Blackcomb Lower Frontside area.
(Source: FATMAP.com)

■ **Merlin's:** Merlin's is an ungroomed, bumpy Blue run under the Blackcomb Gondola. It starts on the right side (looking downhill) of Upper Mainline (Blue), crosses Green Line (Green), and ends near the end of Lower Cruiser (Blue).

NOTE: Although this is designated as a Blue by Whistler Blackcomb, it is ungroomed and bumpy and can be quite challenging depending on the snow conditions. Think of it as a dark Blue verging on a Black run.

■ **School Marm:** School Marm is a short, narrower Blue run that leads from Green Line (Green) through a forested area parallel to the Blackcomb Gondola and then ends on Green Line.

■ **Shorthorn:** Shorthorn is a short Blue run that goes from the bottom of the Excelerator Express Chairlift, under the Excalibur Gondola, and then connects with Lower Cruiser (Blue). This run allows people at the base of the Excelerator Express Chairlift to ski downhill instead of having to traverse up and across to the start of Lower Cruiser.

■ **Upper Mainline:** Upper Mainline is a short Blue run with some steep sections that runs from just above the Blackcomb Gondola Mid Station down to Green Line (Green). You can often find a short, fun mogul field on the left side of this run just below the Blackcomb Gondola Mid Station.

Black Runs/Areas

There are no Black runs on Blackcomb Lower Frontside.

Other Areas

■ **Homerun:** Home Run is a ski-out trail that leads to some of the buildings in the Blackcomb Upper Benchlands. Homerun zigzags down through the forest beside Lower Cruiser (Blue). As you ski down Lower Cruiser you will see several entry points into Home Run along the right side (looking downhill). Locals who know where they are going use this run to ski out to their homes in this area. If you are a visitor renting accommodation in this area, check with the lodging's owner or host to see if it is possible to use this run to ski out to your rental. Make sure that you have clear instructions on how to get to your place so that you do not get lost. Watch for signs with the name of your building or complex.

BLACKCOMB MOUNTAIN

Upper Frontside Area

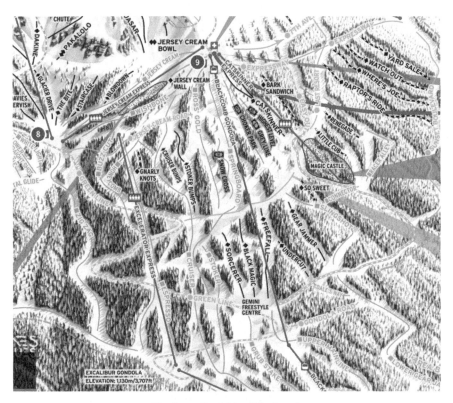

The Upper Frontside of Blackcomb.
(Source: 2022/23 Whistler Blackcomb Trail Map)

The Blackcomb Upper Frontside is the area on Blackcomb above the Blackcomb Gondola Mid Station and the top of the Excalibur Gondola, and below Rendezvous Lodge. This area is accessible via the Excelerator Express Chairlift and the top section of the Blackcomb Gondola.

The Blackcomb Upper Frontside includes a main Green run, numerous Blue runs, and some short Black runs. This is a great area for advanced beginners, intermediate, and even expert skiers.

Locals' Tips

- With its tree-lined runs, the Blackcomb Upper Frontside area is a good option to consider if the weather/visibility is poor higher up in the alpine zone.
- Following runs down from the top of Blackcomb Upper and down into Lower Frontside, and all the way down to Blackcomb base can be a great way to do laps. You can then use the Blackcomb Gondola to get back up the mountain again.
- On a fresh snow/powder day, explore the Blue and Black runs of Upper Frontside for some great fresh tracks and powder lines.

Gondolas/Lifts

Blackcomb Gondola: This is the new eight-person gondola that runs from the Blackcomb base up to the Rendezvous Lodge. The gondola slows down to allow entry/exit about halfway up the front side of Blackcomb at the Blackcomb Gondola Mid Station.

Excelerator Express Chairlift: This is the four-person chair that starts at the top of the Excalibur Gondola and runs to a ridge about halfway between Rendezvous Lodge (above) and Glacier Creek Lodge (below).

Lodges/Huts

Rendezvous Lodge: Rendezvous Lodge is the main lodge at the top of Blackcomb Upper Frontside area. On the main level, it offers a cafeteria with a range of food and drink options, a coffee shop, and plentiful seating with great views of the surrounding mountains. There is also a small outdoor patio on the main level as well as Christine's-on-Blackcomb (a sit-down restaurant—reservations recommended). The lower level includes a small shop, washrooms, and a lower sitting area normally reserved for ski school participants.

Main Routes

Expressway – Easy Out – Green Line: This is the main Green route that runs down Blackcomb Upper Frontside. It starts at the Rendezvous Lodge area, goes down a short section of Expressway, turns down Easy Out, and then turns onto Green Line. Green Line then runs down to the bottom of the Excelerator Express Chairlift (and continues down to the Blackcomb base if you want to go all the way to the bottom).

■ **Wishbone – Cruiser:** This is the main Blue route down Blackcomb Upper Frontside. It starts with Wishbone (just below the Rendezvous Lodge), runs down to where Cruiser starts on the left side of Wishbone, and then follows Cruiser down to the bottom of the Excelerator Express Chairlift.

There is no main Black route down Blackcomb Upper Frontside.

Green Runs

● **Easy Out:** Easy Out is a long, winding Green run that starts on the right side (looking downhill) of Expressway (Green), curves through the Catskinner Express Chairlift area, and ends on Green Line (Green) just above the Blackcomb Gondola Mid Station.

NOTE: The top part of Easy Out around the Catskinner Express Chairlift is heavily used by the ski school as an easy area for beginner lessons.

● **Gondola Road:** Gondola Road is a short, narrow Green run that starts on the right side (looking downhill) of Lower Gear Jammer (Blue) and runs over to the Blackcomb Gondola Mid Station area. It provides a handy 'exit' from Lower Gear Jammer if you want to exit this steep Blue and/or if you want to get to the mid station area.

● **Green Line:** Green Line is a narrow, flat Green run that zigzags down the Blackcomb Upper Frontside. It starts at the Glacier Creek Lodge area and runs down to the bottom of the Excelerator Express Chairlift before continuing down into Blackcomb Lower Frontside. Green Line has a short side leg (the Green Line Connector) that runs from Easy Out (Green) across the bottom of the expert terrain park and Ross's Gold (Blue) and Springboard (Blue) to connect with the main part of Green Line. Green Line is the easiest route down this area and also provides exit points to many runs if you want to head elsewhere on the Blackcomb Upper Frontside.

● **Jersey Cream Road:** Jersey Cream Road is a narrow Green run from Ross's Gold (Blue) across Cruiser (Blue), Honeycomb (Blue), and Buzzcut (Blue), ending on the side of Wishbone (Blue) near the Glacier Creek Lodge area. This run lets you ski the top parts of these Blue runs and then still return to the Jersey Cream Express Chairlift area.

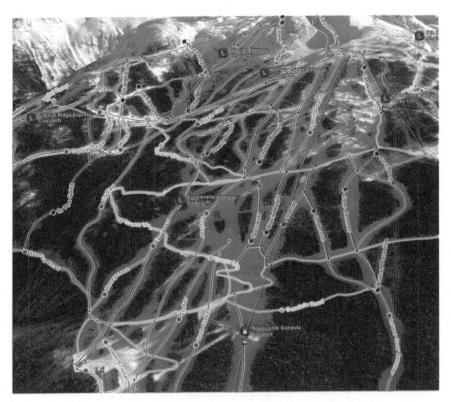

Blackcomb Upper Frontside Green runs including Green Line and Easy Out.
(Source: FATMAP.com)

Blue Runs

■ **Buzz Cut:** Buzz Cut is medium-wide Blue run with some steeper sections that leads from Jersey Cream (Blue) past the top of the Excelerator Express Chairlift and then down to Green Line (Green).

> **NOTE**: Where Buzz Cut passes the top of the Excelerator Express Chairlift, it can get quite busy with people offloading from the chairlift. Slow down to make sure you get past this area safely.

■ **Cruiser:** Cruiser is one of the main, wide Blue runs down the Blackcomb Frontside. Cruiser starts on Wishbone (Blue), curves across the front side, and then ends at the base of the Excelerator Express Chairlift. Below the chairlift, it turns into Lower Cruiser (Blue), which leads down to end on Green Line (Green) near the Blackcomb base.

Max and Meredith Block exploring the trees between Buzz Cut and Zig Zag.
(Source: Jaye Block)

■ **Cruiser Bumps:** Cruiser Bumps is short Black mogul run that starts on the left side (looking downhill) of Cruiser and runs parallel to it. When there is fresh snow, this can be quite a fun, bumpy run.

■ **Espresso:** Espresso consists of several ungroomed, bumpy Blue sections under the Excelerator Express Chairlift. On a fresh snow day, these are great for fresh tracks first thing in the morning.

NOTE: Espresso crosses several Green and Blue runs. Watch out for and avoid other skiers as you make these crossings.

■ **Grubstake:** Grubstake is a short Blue run that starts at the intersection of Green Line (Green) and Stoker (Blue), crosses Green Line (Green), and ends on Lower Cruiser (Blue). If you want to go to the bottom of the Excelerator Express Chairlift, take Stoker or Cruiser, as Grubstake goes past the bottom of the chairlift and down into the Blackcomb Lower Frontside area.

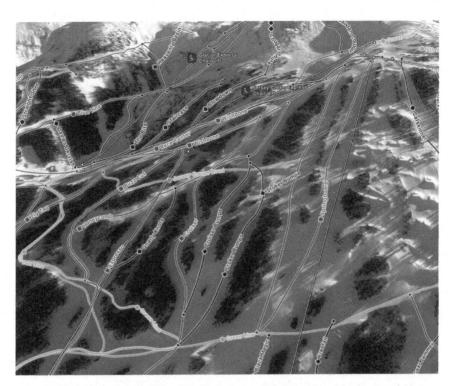

The 'big' Blues—Springboard, Ross's Gold, Cruiser, and Honeycomb—of the Blackcomb Upper Frontside. (Source: FATMAP.com)

■ **Honeycomb:** Honeycomb is medium-wide Blue run that starts on Wishbone just past the start of Cruiser (Blue). It runs parallel to Cruiser down the front side and ends where Blackcomb Glacier Road (Blue) and Green Line (Green) meet just above the Excelerator Express Chairlift base area. Although Honeycomb is normally groomed, the top part of this run can offer some wonderful powder lines on a fresh snow day.

■ **Lower Gear Jammer:** Lower Gear Jammer is a steep Blue run that starts below Easy Out (Green) and runs down into the Blackcomb Lower Frontside. It ends on Green Line (Green) just above the Blackcomb Tube Park. You can exit Lower Gear Jammer on the right just below where it starts and take Gondola Road (Green) over to the Blackcomb Gondola Mid Station area.

■ **Ross's Gold:** Ross's Gold is a wide Blue with steep sections that starts below Rendezvous Lodge on the left side of Wishbone (Blue) and runs down to Green Line (Green).

NOTE: This run is regularly used for ski race training, so it is often closed to the public.

■ **Slingshot:** Slingshot a short, steep Blue run that starts on Green Line (Green) and ends on Easy Out (Green). It is normally groomed but tends to become icy with use. Rumor has it that it gets its name because it feels like you have been shot out of a 'slingshot' when you come around the steep corner in the middle of this run. Slingshot turns into Lower Gear Jammer (Blue) after you cross over Easy Out.

■ **Springboard:** Similar to Ross's Gold (Blue), Springboard is a big, wide blue with steep sections. It starts just below the top of the Blackcomb Gondola, runs down to and crosses Green Line (Green), and then continues down between Cruiser (Blue) and Stoker (Blue) to end on Green Line. With fresh snow or when it is well groomed, this is an amazing carving run and one of my all-time favorites for steep carving laps.

NOTE: Due to heavy use or because of thaw/freeze cycles, this run can be very hard and icy and should then be considered a dark, dark Blue (verging on Black) run.

■ **Stoker:** Stoker is a Blue run that starts on the left side (looking downhill) of Green Line (Green) just below Stoker Bumps (Black). It runs down to end on Green Line near the bottom of the Excelerator Express Chairlift.

HISTORY NOTES

Ross Rebagliati

Ross Rebagliati (born July 14, 1971) is a Canadian snowboarder who won a gold medal in the men's giant slalom event at the 1998 Winter Olympics. The International Olympic Committee initially stripped him of the medal due to a failed drug test for cannabis use but was overruled by an appeals court two days later, resulting in the medal being restored. Since retiring from snowboarding, Rebagliati has become an entrepreneur in the cannabis industry.

Ross's Gold is named after him to honor his gold-medal win at the Olympics.

Source: https://en.wikipedia.org/wiki/Ross_Rebagliati

■ **Stoker Bumps:** Stoker Bumps is a short Black mogul run that starts on the right side (looking downhill) of Ross's Gold (Blue) and runs down to Green Line (Green). You can also access this run from the left side (looking downhill) of Cruiser Bumps (Black). The first part of Stoker Bumps is quite flat, and the middle to end is steep with medium to large moguls. With fresh snow, this can be a fun, bumpy run.

■ **Wishbone:** Wishbone is a medium-wide Blue that starts below Rendezvous Lodge and runs down towards the base of the Jersey Cream Express Chairlift. It gets its name because it splits into two runs (like a chicken wishbone) around several forest 'islands'. Each of the two ends go down to the bottom of the Jersey Cream Express Chairlift.

> **NOTE:** Due to heavy use, this run can get skied out and become icy and/or bumpy as the day goes along.

■ **Zig Zag:** Zig Zag is a medium-wide Blue run with some steep sections that starts at the Glacier Creek Lodge area and runs down to Blackcomb Glacier Road (near the base of the Excelerator Express Chairlift). It is the leftmost run (looking uphill) in the Blackcomb Upper Frontside area.

Black Runs/Areas

> **NOTE:** Watch for and avoid tree wells in all the glade areas described below! If you are skiing in the glades, ski with a partner who can assist you in case you do go into a tree well.

◆ **Black Magic:** Black Magic is one of the steep Black mogul runs on the Blackcomb Upper Frontside. It starts on Green Line (Green), runs parallel with Sorcerer (Black) and Freefall (Black), and ends at the bottom on Easy Out (Green) just above the Blackcomb Gondola Mid Station. With fresh, carvable snow, this can be quite a fun run.

> **NOTE:** Given its location mid mountain, this run and its Black siblings are prone to thaw/freeze cycles and can become quite icy.

◆ **Freefall:** Freefall is a slightly longer version of Black Magic (Black), running from Green Line (Green), under the Blackcomb Gondola, and down to Easy Out (Green).

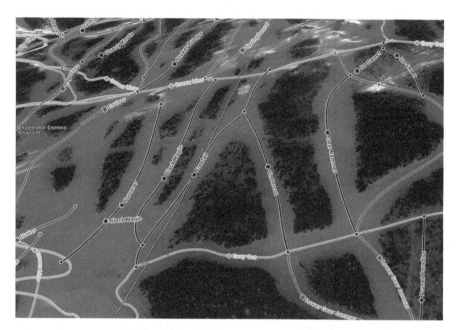

The bumpy Black runs in the middle of the Blackcomb Upper Frontside area including Undercut, Freefall, Sorcerer, and Black Magic. (Source: FATMAP.com)

◆ **Upper Gear Jammer:** Upper Gear Jammer is the shortest of the Black mogul runs on the Blackcomb Upper Frontside. It is the leftmost run (looking downhill) and runs from Green Line (Green) down to Easy Out (Green).

◆ **Gnarly Knots:** Gnarly Knots is a short Black glade area that starts on the left side (looking downhill) of Honeycomb (Blue), runs parallel to Espresso (Blue), and ends on Espresso. This run has steep sections, and the trees can be quite tight (it is definitely 'gnarly').

◆ **Pruned Paradise:** Pruned Paradise is a short section of tight Black glades that runs from Easy Out (Green) down to Lower Gear Jammer (Blue). This area was cleared out (pruned) by Whistler Blackcomb to open it up for glade skiing.

◆ **So Sweet:** So Sweet is a short Black glade area that starts on the Green Line Connector (Green) at the bottom of the Blackcomb Terrain Park, crosses Connector (Green), and ends on Slingshot (Blue). This glade run can be 'so sweet' with powder on fresh snow days.

◆ **Sorcerer:** Sorcerer is a steep Black mogul run similar to Black Magic (Black) and Freefall (Black). It starts on Green Line (Green) at the top and runs down to Easy Out (Green) at the bottom. With fresh snow, this can be a fun, bumpy run.

> **NOTE**: The bottom half of this run is normally closed to the public, as it is used for freestyle jump practice. You can ski up to the side of this area and watch the freestyle kids jump onto a big airbag.

◆ **Undercut:** Undercut is a short, steep Black mogul run similar to Freefall (Black) and Black Magic (Black). It starts on the left side (looking downhill) of Freefall (Black), crosses Easy Out (Green), and ends down on Lower Gear Jammer (Blue).

Other Areas

Unmarked Runs and Glades: There are many unmarked glade areas and short connector runs throughout Blackcomb Upper Frontside. These provide plenty of opportunity for exploring and moving between runs.

> **NOTE**: As with any unmarked area, skiing these areas should be approached with caution until you are familiar with them. Watch and obey all warning signs (for example, cliff warnings) in order to avoid dangerous terrain.

BLACKCOMB MOUNTAIN

Catskinner Express Chairlift Area

The Catskinner area of Blackcomb.
(Source: 2022/23 Whistler Blackcomb Trail Map)

The Catskinner Express Chairlift area is located between the Blackcomb Upper Frontside and the 7th Heaven Express Chairlift areas. The Catskinner area includes Green, Blue, and some Black runs and glades, including the Catskinner (Black) run that shares its name with the chairlift. This area is also home to the Blackcomb Magic Castle, a castle-like structure with slides for younger kids.

This area is popular with a range of skiers and snowboarders. It is heavily used by the ski school for youth and beginner lessons given the Green runs in this area. Freestyle skiers and snowboarders who want to ski the Blackcomb Terrain Park also use the Catskinner

Express Chairlift. Finally, freeride skiers looking for challenging glade runs will explore the Black glades in this area.

The Catskinner run and chairlift get their name from the snowcat and caterpillar tractor operators who were nicknamed 'cat skinners'. Before the Blackcomb Gondola (and previous chairlifts that serviced this area) were installed, the Catskinner Express Chairlift was the highest chairlift on Blackcomb.

Locals' Tips

- It can be fun to watch skiers and snowboarders do jumps and tricks in the Blackcomb Terrain Park, but this should be done from a safe distance (either from Springboard or Catskinner runs). Don't ski into the park unless you understand how to ski in this area and avoid getting in the way.
- While waiting for the 7th Heaven area to open, many locals will do some warm-up laps in the Catskinner area.

Gondolas/Lifts

Catskinner Express Chairlift: This is the short, four-person chair that runs from the bottom of the Blackcomb Terrain Park up to the Rendezvous Lodge area.

Lodges/Huts

Rendezvous Lodge: Rendezvous Lodge is the lodge near the top of the Catskinner Express Chairlift. On the main level, it offers a cafeteria with a range of food and drink options, a coffee shop, and plenty of seating with great views of the surrounding mountains. There is also a small outdoor patio on the main level as well as Christine's-on-Blackcomb (a sit-down restaurant—reservations recommended). The lower level includes a small shop, washrooms, and a lower sitting area normally reserved for ski school participants.

Main Routes

● **Expressway – Easy Out:** This is the main Green route in this area. Expressway starts near the top of the Catskinner Express Chairlift and runs down to Easy Out, which then goes down to the

Catskinner Express Chairlift base area.

There are no main Blue or Black routes in this area.

Green Runs

The Lower Catskinner area with its Green, Blue, and Black runs.
(Source: FATMAP.com)

● **Big Easy:** Big Easy is a medium-wide Green run that starts on the left side (looking downhill) of Easy Out (Green) and goes down to the Catskinner Express Chairlift base area. It is an alternative route to Easy Out to get to the bottom of the chair.

● **Easy Out:** Easy Out is a long Green run that starts on the right side of Expressway (Green), curves towards the terrain park area, goes under the Catskinner Express Chairlift, and then turns back down to the bottom of the chairlift. Easy Out continues downhill and ends near the Blackcomb Gondola Mid Station. This is the main Green run used by the ski school for beginner and children's lessons.

● **Expressway:** Expressway is one of the two Green runs that lead down to the bottom of the 7th Heaven Express Chairlift. It starts near the top of the Catskinner Express Chairlift (where it is quite flat and wide) and then narrows down as it progresses around the mountain over to the 7th Heaven area.

● **Green Line Connector:** The Green Line Connector is a side arm of Green Line (Green). It starts on the right side (looking downhill) of Easy Out (Green) at the base of the Blackcomb Terrain Park. It then runs across the Blackcomb Upper Frontside to join with the main part of Green Line where it meets with Cruiser (Blue).

● **Last Resort:** Last Resort is a long, narrow Green run that starts in the middle of the 7th Heaven area and runs into the Catskinner Express Chairlift area where it joins with Easy Out (Green).

Blue Runs

■ **Connector:** Connector is a narrow Blue run from the base of the Catskinner Express Chairlift over to Slingshot (Blue), which then leads downhill into the Blackcomb Lower Frontside area.

■ **Countdown:** Countdown is a short, medium-wide Blue run with a slightly steep first section. It starts on Easy Out (Green), crosses Last Resort (Green), and curves down to end on Big Easy (Green). This run is used by the ski school to teach beginners how to handle slightly steeper slopes.

■ **Racer Alley:** Racer Alley is a short Blue run that starts on the left side of Countdown (Blue) and ends on Big Easy (Green).

NOTE: The end of this run is flat and slightly uphill, so keep up your speed and/or be ready to walk/skate to the end of the run.

■ **Slingshot:** Slingshot is a short, steep Blue run that starts on Green Line (Green) just below the bottom of the Blackcomb Terrain Park and ends on Easy Out (Green).

NOTE: Although Slingshot is indicated as a Blue run, if it gets icy it can be a very dark Blue (leaning towards Black).

Black Runs/Areas

NOTE: Watch for and avoid tree wells in all the glade areas described below! If you are skiing in the glades, ski with a partner who can assist you in case you do go into a tree well.

Some of the Black glade runs in the Catskinner area.
(Source: FATMAP.com)

◆ **Bark Sandwich:** Bark Sandwich is a difficult Black glade run that starts on Expressway (Green), runs parallel to Catskinner (Black), and ends on Easy Out (Green).

> **NOTE**: This is definitely an expert glade run with steep sections, tight trees, and big bumps. Be careful at the end of this run where you exit onto Easy Out, as it is often packed with kids and beginner skiers.

◆ **Catskinner:** Catskinner is a wide, steep Black run that is normally groomed but becomes a mogul run with heavy use. It starts on the right side (looking downhill) of Expressway (Green) and runs down to end on Easy Out (Green).

> **NOTE**: The moguls on this run can be quite large and challenging. Given its orientation on the mountain, Catskinner is also prone to thaw/freeze cycles and can be quite icy at times.

◆ **Little Cub:** Little Cub is a short Black glade run with an easier slope and spaced-out trees. It starts on Easy Out (Green) and ends on Big Easy (Green). Little Cub and Renegade (Black) are often overlooked and can offer hidden patches of powder on a fresh snow day.

♦ **Renegade:** Similar to Little Cub, Renegade is a short Black glade run in the 'tree island' between Big Easy (Green) and Countdown (Blue). It starts on Last Resort (Green) and ends on Countdown (Blue).

♦ **So Sweet:** So Sweet is a short, steep Black glade area below the Green Line Connector (Green) and above Slingshot (Blue). This glade can be 'so sweet' with powder on fresh snow days.

NOTE: This is definitely an expert glade run with tight trees.

♦ **Upper Gear Jammer:** Upper Gear Jammer is a short Black mogul run that starts from Green Line (Green) and goes down to Easy Out (Green).

Other Areas

Blackcomb Terrain Park: The Blackcomb Terrain Park starts just below the top of the Catskinner Express Chairlift, runs down parallel to Springboard (Blue) and Catskinner (Black), and ends at the bottom on Easy Out (Green). This terrain park includes medium, large, and extra-large features and is designed for intermediate and expert park skiers.

For more information, visit https://www.whistler.com/skiing/terrain-parks/.

NOTE: Before you go into a terrain park, read all the signs at the entrance to the park. Freestyle skiing comes with a greater risk, and you must understand what steps to take to make the park safe for you and everyone around you. If you are unsure, watch a video, ask an experienced rider, or consider booking a park lesson. For more information about terrain park safety, check out: https://www.whistlerblackcomb.com/the-mountain/more-options/safety.aspx

Blackcomb Magic Castle: The Magic Castle is a fun, castle-like structure for younger kids in the forest below Easy Out (Green) and above the bottom of the Catskinner Express Chairlift. You can access the castle from the left side (looking downhill) of Easy Out (Green). There are two entrances: the first leads down a path that is a bit more difficult (Blue), and the second leads down an easier path (Green) for smaller kids or beginners. The castle has different sections, some bridges, and some slides for kids to explore. The exit from the castle is via a Green path down to the bottom of the Catskinner Express Chairlift.

NOTE: There are no washrooms at the castle, so keep this in mind for your kids. The nearest washrooms are up in Rendezvous Lodge.

Blackcomb Magic Castle seen from the Catskinner Express Chairlift.
(Source: Marc Gault)

Jersey Cream Express Chairlift Area

The Jersey Cream area of Blackcomb. (Source: FATMAP.com)

The Jersey Cream Express Chairlift area is located in the central mid-mountain area of Blackcomb and is one of the first upper chairlifts to open on Blackcomb every day. After uploading either via the Blackcomb Gondola or the Excelerator Express Chairlift, you can do some warm-up laps on the runs in this area before heading to other parts of the mountain. You can also go into Rendezvous Lodge or Glacier Creek Lodge to get a coffee and pastry if you need a morning energy boost or to warm up.

Given its easier Blue runs, including Wishbone and Jersey Cream, the Jersey Cream area is well suited for advanced beginners and intermediates. Experts can head to Jersey Cream Wall and the three large Black mogul runs on the uphill side of this area.

From the Jersey Cream Express Chairlift area, you can access:

- Blackcomb Frontside runs and lifts
- Catskinner Express Chairlift area
- Runs over to the 7th Heaven Express Chairlift
- Glacier Express Chairlift area
- Crystal Ridge Express Chairlift area

Locals' Tips

- The top of the Jersey Cream Express Chairlift is in the alpine zone above the tree line, so it can be a bit challenging if visibility is poor. If this is the case, I recommend turning right at the top of the chair and heading towards the Rendezvous Lodge area, where you will start to get back into tree-lined runs.
- On a fresh snow day, before the higher alpine lifts open, there is often fresh powder on the top sections of Buzz Cut, Cruiser, and Honeycomb. You can then take the Excelerator Express Chairlift back up to the Jersey Cream area.
- The area of the Jersey Cream Wall under the chairlift offers some good intermediate moguls on which to ski and/or practice.
- There are numerous unmarked glade areas between the runs in the Jersey Cream area. Watch for locals leading the way into these glades or ask someone who knows their way around to show you what paths to take through the glades.

Gondolas/Lifts

Jersey Cream Express Chairlift: This is the four-person chair that runs from the Glacier Creek Lodge area up to above the Rendezvous Lodge area.

Lodges/Huts

Glacier Creek Lodge: Glacier Creek Lodge is a large, two-level lodge at the base of the Jersey Cream Express and the Glacier Express Chairlifts. The main cafeteria and coffee bar on the second floor offer food and drinks with ample seating. There is also a small snack bar on the lower level with additional seating inside and outside. The lodge has a small shop as well as washrooms on the first floor.

Glacier Creek Lodge with the Jersey Cream Express Chairlift on the left and the Glacier Express Chairlift on the right. (Source: Nick Jones)

Rendezvous Lodge: Rendezvous Lodge is the lodge at the top of the Blackcomb Gondola. On the main level, it offers a cafeteria with a range of food and drink options, a coffee shop, and plenty of seating with great views of the surrounding mountains. There is also a small outdoor patio on the main level as well as Christine's-on-Blackcomb (a sit-down restaurant—reservations recommended). The lower level includes a small shop, washrooms, and a lower sitting area normally reserved for ski school participants.

Main Routes

There is no main Green route in this area.

■ **Jersey Cream:** The Jersey Cream run is one of the two main Blue routes down through the Jersey Cream area. It starts on the left at the top of the Jersey Cream Express Chairlift and runs down into the Jersey Cream Bowl before curving down to the bottom of the Jersey Cream Express Chairlift.

■ **Wishbone:** Wishbone is the other main Blue route through this area. Wishbone starts beside the Rendezvous Lodge, runs along the top of Jersey Cream Wall, and then splits into two routes that run down to the bottom of the Jersey Cream Express Chairlift. Of the two main Blue routes, Wishbone is the easier one.

There is no main Black route in this area.

Meredith Block about to head down the Jersey Cream Race Center next to Cougar Milk.
(Source: Jaye Block)

Green Runs

🟢 **Jersey Cream Road:** Jersey Cream Road is a narrow Green path that runs from Ross's Gold (Blue) across Cruiser (Blue), Honeycomb (Blue), and Buzzcut (Blue) before ending on the side of Wishbone (Blue) near the bottom of the Jersey Cream Express Chairlift. This run allows you to ski the upper sections of Ross's Gold, Cruiser, Honeycomb, and Buzzcut, and still return to the bottom of the Jersey Cream Express Chairlift (versus heading down into the Blackcomb Upper Frontside area).

Blue Runs

The Blue runs in the Jersey Cream Express Chairlift area including the Jersey Cream run and Wishbone. (Source: FATMAP.com)

Buzz Cut: Buzz Cut is medium-wide Blue with some steeper sections that runs from Jersey Cream Run (Blue) past the top of the Excelerator Express Chairlift and then down to Green Line (Green). On a fresh powder day, the top of this run can offer some great fresh tracks.

Cougar Milk: Cougar Milk is steeper Blue that starts on the right side (looking downhill) of Wishbone (Blue) and then curves down to the bottom of the Jersey Cream Express Chairlift. The Jersey Cream Race Center runs down the left side of Cougar Milk.

Cruiser: Cruiser is one of the main Blues that runs down the Blackcomb Frontside from Wishbone (Blue). It curves across the frontside and ends near the bottom of the Excelerator Express Chairlift. Similar to Buzz Cut, the top of this run can offer some great skiing on a fresh powder day.

Honeycomb: Honeycomb is a Blue that starts on Wishbone just past where Cruiser (Blue) starts. It runs parallel to Cruiser down the frontside and ends where Blackcomb Glacier Road (Blue) and Green Line (Green) meet just above the bottom of the Excelerator Express Chairlift.

Jersey Cream: The Jersey Cream run is one of the two main Blue runs that lead down from the top of the Jersey Cream Express Chairlift to its bottom. This run is normally groomed and has some steep sections. You can access this run to the left when you get off at the top of the Jersey Cream Express.

NOTE: Due to heavy use, this run can get skied out and become icy and/or bumpy as the day goes on. Given that this run is in the open alpine of the lower Jersey Cream, it can also be challenging when visibility is poor.

Nick's Bumps: Nick's Bumps is a short Blue mogul run that starts on the side of Wishbone (Blue) and goes down to Jersey Cream (Blue). This is a great short stretch of moguls and can be wonderful when there is fresh snow. This set of bumps is also a good location to start to learn how to ski moguls (it is where I learned).

Ross's Gold: Ross's Gold is a big Blue run with steep sections that starts below Rendezvous Lodge on the left side (looking downhill) of Wishbone (Blue) and runs down to Green Line (Green).

NOTE: This run is often closed to the public when it is being used for ski race training.

Heading up the Jersey Cream Express Chairlift with Jersey Cream (Blue) below on a fresh snow day. (Source: Susan Rogers)

■ Wishbone: Wishbone is a Blue run from below Rendezvous Lodge down to the bottom of the Jersey Cream Express Chairlift. It gets its name because it splits into two runs (like a chicken's wishbone) around several forest 'islands'. Each of the two ends go down to the Jersey Cream Express Chairlift base/Glacier Creek Lodge area. It is normally groomed and has some steeper sections.

NOTE: Due to heavy use, this run can get skied out and become icy and/or bumpy as the day goes on.

Black Runs/Areas

◆ **Baggers:** The Baggers is a Black area of boulder-strewn open alpine with some trees below Cougar Chutes (Black) and above Coyote Road (Blue). You can access this area by traversing off-piste near the top of Jersey Cream run (Blue) and following along as high as possible below the cliffs above and to the right. The other way to access this area is from Cougar Chutes above.

◆ **Blowdown:** Blowdown is a bumpy Black run from Coyote Road (Blue) down to Jersey Cream (Blue). You can access it by turning right off Jersey Cream Run (Blue) onto Coyote Road and then turning left onto Blowdown. Blowdown is the easier of the three black mogul runs along this side of Jersey Cream run. It is sometimes groomed but can become bumpy with use.

The Jersey Cream Express Chairlift with Glacier Drive, The Bite, Staircase, and Blowdown (left to right) in the background. (Source: Susan Rogers)

◆ **Cafe Chute:** Cafe Chute is the small, steep Black chute in the middle of the Jersey Cream cliffs. When going up on the Jersey Cream Express Chairlift, watch for young rippers showing their stuff coming down this chute. You can access this chute from the right side (looking downhill) of Wishbone (Blue).

> **NOTE**: Plan your route down this chute carefully, as the area below the chute is quite flat and can make for a challenging landing.

♦ **Glacier Drive:** Glacier Drive is a Black run down from Blue Line (Blue) to the bottom of the Glacier Creek Express Chairlift.

> **NOTE**: This run is normally groomed but can become icy and bumpy due to heavy traffic as people use it to exit the Glacier Express Chairlift area.

♦ **Jersey Cream Wall:** Jersey Cream Wall is a bumpy Black slope below the top of the Jersey Cream Express Chairlift. It is less steep on the right (looking downhill) and steeper on the left. The whole Jersey Cream Wall can be quite wonderful with fresh snow and is a locals' favorite for bumpy warm-up runs at the beginning of the day.

> **NOTE**: Given its popularity, the wall can get skied out and icy with use.

Jersey Cream Wall in the foreground with the Lower Feather Tree, the Saudan Couloir, and Chainsaw Ridge in the background. (Source: Nick Jones)

♦ **Pumphouse Roll:** Pumphouse Roll is the small Black roll just to the right (looking downhill) of Jersey Cream cliffs. You can access this roll from the right side (looking downhill) of Wishbone (Blue). It gets its name from the pump house buildings below it.

♦ **K Bumps:** The K Bumps is a short, steep set of Black moguls on the far-left side of the Jersey Cream cliffs next to Tree Fall (Black). You can access this run from the right side (looking downhill) of Wishbone (Blue).

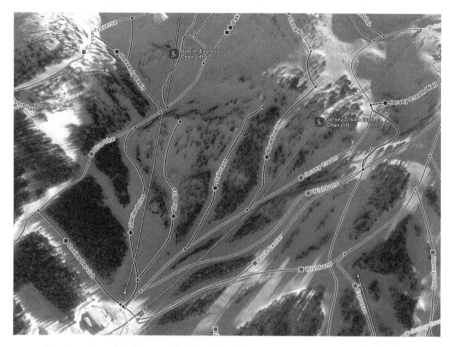

The three large Black runs—The Bite, Staircase, and Blowdown—on the east side of the Jersey Cream area below Cougar Chutes. (Source: FATMAP.com)

♦ **Staircase:** Staircase is a steep, challenging Black mogul run that comes down from Coyote Road (Blue) and ends on Wishbone (Blue). You can access it by turning right off Jersey Cream (Blue) onto Coyote Road and then turning left onto Staircase.

> **NOTE**: This is a steep, challenging mogul run that can have large, deep moguls. I recommend only approaching this when there is either a decent amount of fresh snow or the snow is soft and carvable. If conditions are icy, this is a good one to avoid.

♦ **The Bite:** The Bite is the third and most difficult steep Black mogul run from Coyote Road (Blue) down to the bottom of the Jersey Cream Express Chairlift. This run is recognizable by the very large boulder in the middle of the lower half of the run. You can access The Bite by turning right (looking downhill) off Jersey Cream Run (Blue) onto Coyote Road and then continuing along until you turn left down onto The Bite.

> **NOTE**: Similar to Staircase, this is a steep, challenging mogul run that can have large, deep moguls. I recommend only approaching this when there is either a decent amount of fresh snow or the snow is soft and carvable.

The Jersey Cream Express Chairlift heading up and over Jersey Cream Wall with 'The Spoon' on the right. (Source: Nick Jones)

♦ **The Spoon:** The Spoon is the small Black bowl just to the right (looking downhill) of Jersey Cream cliffs. You can access this bowl from the right side (looking downhill) of Wishbone (Blue). The Spoon gets its name from its shape, which resembles the shape of the cup at the end of a spoon.

♦ **Tree Fall:** Tree Fall Chute is a small Black chute squeezed between the trees on the far left (looking downhill) of the Jersey Cream cliffs. You can access this chute from the right side (looking downhill) of Wishbone (Blue).

NOTE: Think about how you plan to go down this chute, as the landing can be quite flat and challenging.

Other Areas

■ **Coyote Road:** Coyote Road is a flat, unmarked Blue cat track that runs from the right side of Jersey Cream (Blue) over to Blue Line (Blue). It provides an exit for The Baggers (Black) and Cougar Chutes (Black) and provides access to Blowdown (Black), Staircase (Black), and The Bite (Black) below it.

♦ **Hooker Hump:** Hooker Hump is an unmarked 'run' that follows along below the Jersey Cream Express Chairlift as it goes over a hump beside Jersey Cream run (Blue). The top part of Hooker Hump is open and exposed with steep sections, and the bottom exits onto Jersey Cream. You can access it by turning right off Jersey Cream (Blue) onto Coyote Road (Blue) and then turning left through the trees to get to Hooker Hump. The path up to the top of the hump is a bit uphill, so it requires some work to get up.

NOTE: Given its location on the mountain, this hump can suffer from thaw/freeze cycles that can make it very icy.

■ **Jersey Cream Race Center:** The Jersey Cream Race Center is a fenced-off portion of Cougar Milk (Blue) that has a small ski racecourse on it. It runs down the left side of Cougar Milk (looking downhill) and ends on Wishbone (Blue). If it is not being used for training or races, you and a friend can run the racecourse side by side and see your times displayed at the bottom.

Heading up and over Hooker Hump on the Jersey Cream Express Chairlift.
(Source: Nick Jones)

◆ **Unmarked Glades:** There are sections of unmarked glades between the runs throughout the Jersey Cream Express Chairlift area. These can be quite fun with fresh snow.

> **NOTE**: Watch for and obey the signs between the Jersey Cream runs that warn of cliffs and creeks. Whenever entering glades, watch for and avoid tree wells.

Spring skiers and boarders heading up the Jersey Cream Express Chairlift with the Coastal Mountains in the background. (Source: Nick Jones)

Crystal Ridge Express Chairlift Area

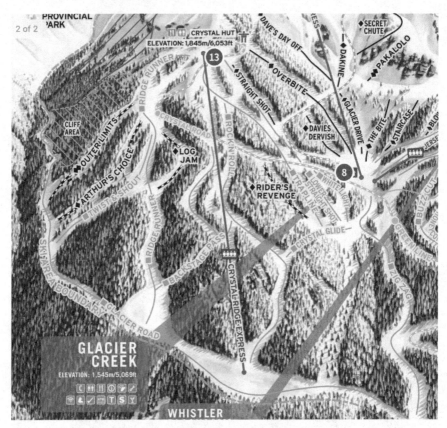

The Crystal Ridge area on Blackcomb. (Source: 2022/23 Whistler Blackcomb Trail Map)

*T*he Crystal Ridge Express Chairlift area is on the northern edge of Blackcomb and offers some great tree-lined Blue runs, Black runs, and Black glade-skiing options. Access to this area is via the Crystal Ridge Express Chairlift, which ends just into the open alpine zone of the mountain. Rumor has it that Crystal Ridge gets its name from the crystal-like powder snow that is often found here on a fresh snow day.

With its Blue and Black runs and off-piste and glade areas, this is a great area for intermediate and expert skiers. There are also challenging unmarked Black runs and glade areas for expert skiers.

Locals' Tips

- If visibility is poor in the higher alpine areas, the Crystal Ridge Express Chairlift area is a good option for tree-lined runs.
- The Crystal Ridge Express Chairlift is well known by locals as a place to go on a fresh snow/powder day. Although most of the runs are groomed, the glades and areas on either side of the runs provide great options for fresh powder tracks.
- On a nice day, the views from the outdoor deck at Crystal Hut are hard to beat. It is a perfect spot for coffee and some of Crystal Hut's famous waffles for an afternoon snack!

Gondolas/Lifts

Crystal Ridge Express Chairlift: This is the four-person chairlift that services the Crystal Ridge Express Chairlift area. You can access the Crystal Ridge Express Chairlift area either via Crystal Traverse (Blue) from the top or at the bottom via Crystal Glide (Blue) from the Glacier Creek Lodge area.

Lodges/Huts

Crystal Ridge Hut: Crystal Ridge Hut is the small hut at the top of the Crystal Ridge Express Chairlift. It offers limited food, snack, and drink options but is famous for its waffles. This hut also has a small outdoor deck with amazing views on a clear day. Sitting on the deck in the afternoon sun is a wonderful way to take a break in the afternoon. There are washrooms in a separate building next to the hut.

Main Routes

Crystal Road: Crystal Road is the main and only Green run in this area. It starts behind the Crystal Ridge Hut, curves underneath it, and then continues to work its way around and down through the Crystal Ridge Express Chairlift area. Crystal Road ends at the Glacier Creek Lodge area where it connects with the top of Green

Line (Green).

Crystal Hut deep in the snow on a bluebird spring day. (Source: Nick Jones)

■ **Ridge Runner:** Ridge Runner is one of the main Blue runs in the Crystal Ridge area. It starts at the top of the Crystal Ridge Express Chairlift and runs down to Blackcomb Glacier Road (Blue), which then leads over to the bottom of the Crystal Ridge Express Chairlift.

■ **Rock'n'Roll:** Rock'n'Roll is the other main Blue run from the top of the Crystal Express Chairlift down through the Crystal Ridge area to the bottom of the chairlift. It starts at the top of the Crystal Ridge Express Chairlift, curves back and forth across the front of this area and ends at the bottom of the Crystal Ridge Express Chairlift.

There is no main Black route through the Crystal Ridge area.

Green Runs

● **Crystal Road:** Crystal Road is the only Green run in the Crystal Ridge Express Chairlift area. It starts behind the Crystal Ridge Hut, curves underneath it, and then continues to wind its way around and down through this area. Crystal Road ends at the Glacier Creek Lodge area where it connects with the top of Green Line (Green).

Blue Runs

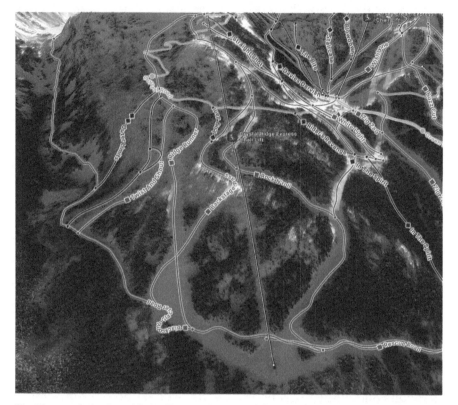

The Blue runs in the Crystal Ridge Express Chairlift area including Ridge Runner, Rock 'n' Roll, and Backstage Pass. (Source: FATMAP.com)

Backstage Pass: Backstage Pass is a Blue run with some steep sections. Normally groomed, it can also offer some nice fresh tracks on a powder day. It starts on the right side (looking downhill) of Rock 'n' Roll (Blue), runs parallel with it, and then curves off to the right to join with Ridge Runner (Blue).

Blackcomb Glacier Road: Blackcomb Glacier Road is the long, narrow Blue run that emerges from the bottom of the Blackcomb Glacier, passes the bottom of the Crystal Ridge Express Chairlift, and continues to the bottom of the Excelerator Express Chairlift. Several of the Crystal Ridge area runs end on Blackcomb Glacier Road.

■ **Crystal Glide:** Crystal Glide is the lower Blue access route into the Crystal Ridge area. It starts near the Glacier Creek Lodge area and ends on Rock 'n' Roll (Blue), which then continues down to the Crystal Express Chairlift base. This run varies in width and has steeper and flatter sections. The first section is flat and slightly uphill, so pick up some speed as you approach it.

NOTE: This run can get skied out and become icy/bumpy due to traffic going down to the bottom of the Crystal Express Chairlift.

■ **Crystal Traverse:** Crystal Traverse is a narrow, relatively flat Blue that is the upper access route into the Crystal Ridge area. It starts at the top of the Glacier Express Chairlift, traverses along the side of the mountain, and ends at the top of the Crystal Express Chairlift.

■ **Lower Straight Shot:** Lower Straight Shot is a Blue run that starts on Blue Line (Blue), runs down to cross Crystal Road (Green) and Blue Line lower down, and then ends at the bottom near the end of White Light (Blue). The exit at the bottom is to the left onto Zig Zag (Blue). This is the lower and easier half of the two 'straight shot' runs that go straight down the mountain below Crystal Hut.

■ **Ridge Runner:** Ridge Runner is one of the main Blue runs that leads from the top of the Crystal Express Chairlift down through the Crystal Ridge area and ends on Blackcomb Glacier Road (Blue). This run varies in width, has some steep sections, and provides access to glades and off-piste sections on either side of the run. On a fresh snow day, either side of the top section of this run can provide very nice powder lines and fluffy bumps.

NOTE: Given that this is a main route, the top and bottom of this run can get skied out and become icy/bumpy due to traffic.

■ **Rock 'n' Roll:** Rock 'n' Roll is the other main Blue run through the Crystal Ridge area. It starts at the top of the Crystal Ridge Express Chairlift, curves down across the front of this area, and ends at the bottom of the Crystal Ridge Express Chairlift. This run has several steep sections and is normally groomed.

NOTE: The top part of this run is part of the main exit route out of the Crystal Ridge area and can get skied out and become icy/bumpy due to traffic as the day progresses.

Crystal Ridge Express Chairlift crossing over Rock 'n' Roll with Green Lake and the Whistler valley in the background. (Source: Nick Jones)

■ **Trapline:** Trapline is a wide Blue run with a couple of steep sections. It starts on the left side of Rock 'n' Roll (Blue), curves downhill, crosses Crystal Road (Green), and ends on Crystal Glide (Blue).

> **NOTE:** The top half of this run is one of the main exit routes out of the Crystal Ridge area, so it can get skied out and become icy/bumpy as the day progresses.

■ **Twist and Shout:** Twist and Shout is a short Blue run with steep sections that runs from the right side (looking downhill) of Ridge Runner (Blue) and ends on Blackcomb Glacier Road (Blue). It is occasionally groomed and often bumpy. When there is fresh snow, this is a locals' favorite for fresh tracks. Twist and Shout runs parallel to Arthur's Choice (Black) and provides easy exits out of that Black glade area.

■ **White Light:** White Light is a Blue mogul run with some steep sections. It starts just below the top of the Crystal Ridge Express Chairlift, crosses Blue Line (Blue) and Crystal Road (Green), and ends below Crystal Glide (Blue). The exit at the bottom is out to the left onto Zig Zag (Blue). White Light runs parallel to Upper and Lower

Straight Shot and is effectively the same run in some sections. With fresh snow, this can be a fabulous, fluffy bump run.

> **NOTE**: This run faces west, so it can suffer from thaw/freeze cycles that can result in large, icy moguls. It is a good idea to check conditions before committing to this run.

An area of burnt trees alongside the Crystal Ridge Express Chairlift next to Backstage Pass. (Source: Nick Jones)

Black Runs/Areas

◆ **Arthur's Choice:** Arthur's Choice is a bumpy Black glade run that starts on the right side (looking downhill) of Ridge Runner (Blue) and runs down to Blackcomb Glacier Drive (Blue). It is the smaller, less difficult sibling of its neighbor, Outer Limits (Double Black). Arthur's Choice runs parallel to Twist and Shout (Blue), which provides opportunities to exit out of this Black glade area. With new snow, this can be a very fun, fluffy bump run!

> **NOTE**: This run can develop large, hard moguls between the trees that can be very challenging. If in doubt, stick to the left side of this run so that you can exit onto Twist and Shout if needed.

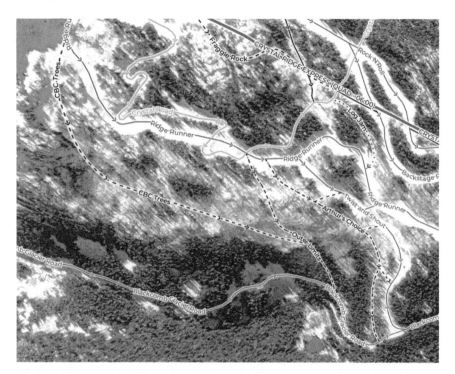

The Black glade runs—CBC Trees, Outer Limits, and Arthur's Choice—on the northwest side of the Crystal Ridge area. (Source: Openskimap.org)

◆ **In the Spirit:** In the Spirit is a long, difficult Black glade run that starts on Crystal Glide (Blue) and ends on Blackcomb Glacier Road (Blue).

> **NOTE**: This run has creek hazards, fallen trees, and other terrain challenges. As a result, it requires a good snow base to make it skiable and enjoyable. If snow conditions are poor, leave this run for another day.

◆ **Log Jam:** Log Jam is a short Black glade run that goes through a section of burnt trees. It starts on the right side (looking downhill) of Crystal Road (Green) and runs down to either exit onto Backstage Pass (Blue) on the left or Ridge Runner (Blue) on the right. With new snow, this can be a fun, relatively easy glade run and is one of my favorite short glade runs on Blackcomb.

◆◆ **Outer Limits:** Outer Limits is a steep, difficult, bumpy Double-Black glade run with tighter trees and big bumps. It starts on the right side (looking downhill) of Ridge Runner (Blue), goes down through an area burnt by a forest fire, and ends on Blackcomb Glacier Drive (Blue). With new snow, many locals consider this one of the best expert glade runs on all of Whistler Blackcomb.

NOTE: Outer Limits is definitely an expert glade zone given the tightness of the trees and many steep sections. It should only be approached when there are good snow conditions.

◆ **Upper Straight Shot:** Upper Straight Shot is a Black mogul run that starts from Crystal Road (Green) just below the Crystal Ridge Hut. It runs parallel to White Light (Blue) and ends on Blueline (Blue). This run is the top part of the two 'straight shot' runs that run straight down the mountain below the Crystal Ridge Hut.

NOTE: This run can develop large, hard moguls, which can be very challenging.

Heading down through the pow in the trees of Outer Limits on a fresh snow day.
(Source: Vanessa Nicole)

◆ **Rider's Revenge:** Rider's Revenge is a short Black glade run that starts on the right side (looking downhill) of Crystal Road (Green) and ends down on Crystal Glide (Blue).

NOTE: As with any glade run, watch for tree wells and ski with a partner.

Other Areas

◆◆ **CBC Trees:** CBC Trees is an unmarked Double-Black glade area below Ridge Runner (Blue) and above Blackcomb Glacier Drive (Blue). The entrance into this area is via a traverse from the right side (looking downhill) near the top of Ridge Runner, and the exit is onto Outer Limits (Double Black). Similar to Outer Limits, locals consider this area some of the best expert glade skiing on Whistler Blackcomb.

NOTE: There is a steep cliff area that runs across the bottom right of CBC Trees area that is dangerous and not skiable. If you choose to ski here, ski towards the left (looking downhill) in the direction of Outer Limits to safely exit this area.

◆◆ **Crystal Ridge Express Chairlift Run:** Underneath the lower half of the Crystal Ridge Express Chairlift is an unmarked run with several steep, difficult sections and cliff faces (Double-Black level in spots). It starts on Rock 'n' roll (Blue) and runs down to Blackcomb Glacier Road (Blue).

NOTE: This run has many logs, stumps, rocks, trees, and other hazards. It should only be attempted when there is sufficient snow cover and only by those with strong off-piste skiing skills.

◆◆ **Fraggle Rock:** Fraggle Rock is a steep, unmarked area that runs down the face of a small summit underneath the Crystal Ridge Express Chairlift. This run is Double-Black level in spots. Starting on Crystal Road (Green) or Rock 'n' Roll (Blue), access to the top of Fraggle Rock is uphill and requires some skating, sidestepping, or a boot hike to get up the back side of the summit. There are several routes down from the summit through burnt trees. All routes lead down to and exit on Crystal Road.

NOTE: The front side of the Fraggle Rock summit can be very exposed and steep and is expert skiing territory. Given the nature of the face, this area can also suffer from a lack of snow due to wind exposure.

◆ **Unmarked Glades:** There are sections of unmarked glades between the runs throughout the Crystal Express Chairlift area. These can be quite fun with fresh snow.

NOTE: Watch for and obey the signs that warn of cliffs, creeks, and other hazards.

Heading up over Fraggle Rock near the top of the Crystal Ridge Express Chairlift.
(Source: Nick Jones)

BLACKCOMB MOUNTAIN

Glacier Express Chairlift Area

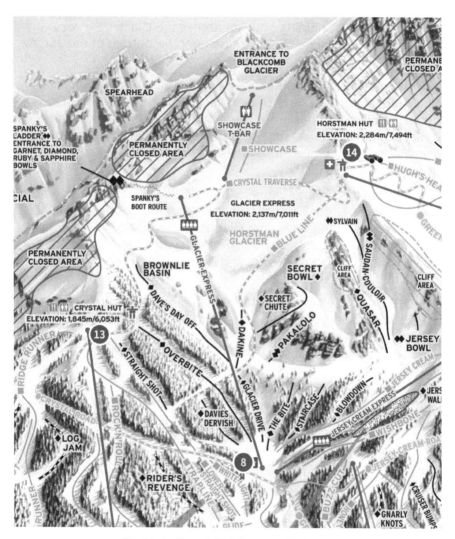

The Glacier Express Chairlift area on Blackcomb.
(Source: 2022/23 Whistler Blackcomb Trail Map)

*T*he Glacier Express Chairlift area is located in the upper alpine zone of Blackcomb in-between the Blackcomb Glacier to the northeast and the 7th Heaven area to the south. Given the terrain, off-piste skiing options, and potential weather conditions, this area should be considered an intermediate and expert skiing zone.

The Glacier Express Chairlift is one of the two chairs on Blackcomb that can take you up into the alpine zone (the other is the 7th Heaven Express Chairlift). You can access the Glacier Express Chairlift next to Glacier Creek Lodge near the bottom of the Jersey Cream Express Chairlift.

This area has plenty of great open alpine skiing options, including Blue Line (quite steep and challenging in some spots), which runs down the middle of this area. There are also many Black skiing options (steeps, bumps, etc.) on either side of this area, including a small bowl—Brownlie Basin (Black)—that can be a lot of fun with good snow and visibility.

At the top of the Glacier Express Chairlift, you can also ski over to the Showcase T-Bar. This will take you up to the boot hike that gives you access into the Blackcomb Glacier (an advanced intermediate and expert skiing zone). You can also follow a traverse over to Spanky's Ladder, boot hike up, and ski into the expert Gemstone Bowls on the other side.

NOTE: Almost all of Glacier is in the alpine, so the area can be very challenging if visibility and/or snow conditions are poor. The bottom of the Glacier Express Chairlift can also be very busy on a good snow day and most weekends, so expect a long wait in line.

Locals' Tips

- On a fresh snow day, the entire Glacier Express Chairlift area can provide wonderful intermediate and expert-level fresh tracks and powder skiing. Showcase and Blueline (Blues) and Brownlie Basin and Dave's Day Off (Black) can be a lot of fun with fresh snow.
- When going up the Glacier Express Chairlift, look to the right side and watch for people coming down chutes and mogul runs from Secret Bowl. On the cliff face to the right, look for the famous The Curl/Lone Pine Run (identifiable by the lone, small pine tree growing on the side of the cliff face) and imagine what it would take to ski down that run.

Gondolas/Lifts

Glacier Express Chairlift: This is the high-speed four-person chair that starts next to the Glacier Creek Lodge and runs up into the alpine zone next to the Horstman Glacier.

Showcase T-Bar: This is the two-person T-bar that runs up the far end of the Glacier Express Chairlift area. It provides access to the boot hike into the Blackcomb Glacier as well as to the top of Showcase (Blue).

Lodges/Huts

There are no lodges or huts up in the Glacier Express Chairlift area.

Main Routes

A skier coming down Blue Line in the morning on a crisp winter day.
(Source: Greg Chen)

There is no main Green route through this area.

■ **Blue Line:** Blue Line is one of the two main Blue runs through this area. Blue Line starts at the top of the ridge behind Horstman Hut, runs down into the Glacier Express Chairlift area, continues down the middle of this area, and then curves down to end behind the Glacier Creek Lodge.

■ **Crystal Traverse:** Crystal Traverse is the other main Blue route through this area. It starts at the top of the Glacier Express Chairlift, curves right and under the chairlift, runs along the side of the mountain, and then ends at the top of the Crystal Ridge Express Chairlift.

There is no main Black route through this area.

Blue Runs

■ **Blue Line:** Blue Line is a long Blue run with steep sections. It is normally groomed but can get bumpy with use. Blue Line starts at the top of the ridge behind Horstman Hut (accessible via the 7th Heaven Express Chairlift), runs down into the Glacier Express Chairlift area, continues down the middle of this area, and then curves down and ends behind Glacier Creek Lodge.

NOTE: Given that this is the main Blue route through the middle of this area, parts of Blue Line can get skied out and icy/bumpy due to heavy traffic.

The Blue runs in the upper part of the Glacier Express Chairlift area including Crystal Traverse, Showcase, and Blue Line. (Source: FATMAP.com)

■ **Crystal Traverse:** Crystal Traverse is a long, relatively flat Blue run. It starts at the top of the Glacier Express Chairlift, curves right and under the chairlift, runs along the side of the mountain, and ends at the top of the Crystal Ridge Express Chairlift. Crystal Traverse has another starting point at the top of the 7th Heaven Express Chairlift that then curves down into the Horstman Glacier Bowl. The main section of Crystal Traverse provides access to a variety of Black runs and areas on either side of the run.

> **NOTE:** The upper part of this run that starts at the top of 7th Heaven is not always groomed and available.

■ **Showcase:** Showcase is a steep, wide Blue run from the top of the Showcase T-Bar down to the bottom of the T-bar. On a fresh snow day, Showcase can provide some amazing steep, fresh tracks.

Looking up at Showcase coming down beside the Showcase T-Bar seen from Blue Line.
(Source: Matteo Schiavon)

Black Runs/Areas

◆ **Brownlie Basin:** Brownlie Basin (also called Heavenly Basin) is a bumpy, cone-shaped Black bowl below Crystal Traverse (Blue) that ends down on Blue Line (Blue). You can drop into this bowl at various points along the left side (looking downhill) of Crystal Traverse. Dave's Day Off (Black) runs down the middle of this basin to Blue Line. This area can be very fun with new snow and good visibility and is one of my favorite bowls on Blackcomb.

> **NOTE:** This bowl faces southwest, so it can suffer from thaw/freeze cycles. Check conditions before committing, or you could be in for a hard ride down this bowl.

◆ **Dakine:** Dakine is a Black mogul field below the Glacier Express Chairlift to the right side (looking downhill) of Blue Line (Blue). If you are going up the chair, you can get a great view of people showing their bump skills coming down this run next to the steep cliff face on the left.

The Black runs in the lower end of the Glacier Express Chairlift area including Davies Dervish, Overbite, Smoked Salmon, and Don't Stop. (Source: Openskimap.org)

◆ **Dave's Day Off:** Dave's Day Off is a bumpy, off-piste Black run that goes down the middle of Brownlie Bowl (Black). This can be a very fun run with new snow and good visibility.

◆ **Davies Dervish:** Davies Dervish is a wide, steep Black mogul run that starts on Blue Line (Blue) and then continues down to the bottom of the Glacier Express Chairlift. Freestyle mogul teams often practice on this run and can be watched from the base area below.

> **NOTE**: This run is known for its large, challenging moguls, so approach it with caution.

◆ **Don't Stop:** Don't Stop is a short, steep Black glade run that is a sibling to Smoked Salmon (Black). This run starts on Crystal Traverse (Blue), curves down through the trees, and ends on Smoked Salmon.

> **NOTE**: This is a challenging, steep glade run with sections of tight trees.

◆ **Glacier Drive:** Glacier Drive is a Black run that drops down from the left (looking downhill) of Blue Line (Blue) and leads down to the bottom of the Glacier Express Chairlift. This run is wider at the top but narrows at its lower end.

> **NOTE**: This run can get icy and bumpy as it gets skied out with traffic heading down to the base area.

◆ **Overbite:** Overbite is a long, steep Black mogul run that starts on Crystal Traverse (Blue), runs down to and crosses Blue Line (Blue), and then continues down to the bottom of the Glacier Express Chairlift.

> **NOTE**: This run is known for its large, challenging moguls, approach with caution.

◆ **Smoked Salmon:** Smoked Salmon is a short, steep Black glade run that starts on Crystal Traverse (Blue), curves down through the trees, and ends on Blue Line (Blue). You can cross Blue Line and continue on Glacier Drive (Black) down to the bottom of the Glacier Express Chairlift.

> **NOTE**: This is a challenging, steep glade run with sections of tight trees.

Other Areas

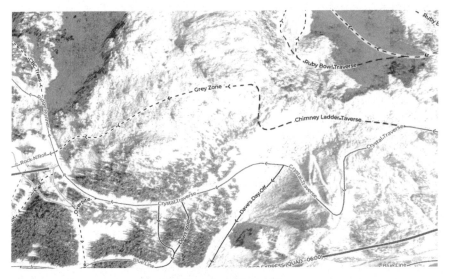

The Grey Zone above Crystal Traverse.
(Source: Openskimap.org)

Looking up at the end of the Grey Zone from the top of the Crystal Ridge Express Chairlift.
(Source: Nick Jones)

Spanky's Ladder leading into the Gemstone Bowls area. (Source: FATMAP.com)

Chimney Ladder: The Chimney Ladder is a lesser-known boot hike (compared to the famous Spanky's Ladder) above Crystal Traverse (Blue). You can access the bottom of this ladder by following the Chimney Ladder Traverse above Crystal Traverse just below the cliffs above and to the right. The traverse ends at the base of a steep boot hike that takes you up to the top of the ridge and into the Grey Zone (Black).

> **NOTE**: This is a difficult, challenging boot hike and should only be attempted by people with the right skills and experience. Ideally, you should go with someone who has done this hike before and can guide the way.

◆ **Grey Zone:** The Grey Zone is a Black area of ungroomed, rocky open alpine high above Crystal Traverse (Blue). It starts at the top of Chimney Ladder and runs down to the top of the Crystal Ridge Express Chairlift.

> **NOTE**: This is an exposed area of alpine that can have a wide range of snow conditions. Watch for boulders and small trees that can catch your skis. This run should only be approached when there is sufficient snow.

Spanky's Ladder: Spanky's Ladder is the famous boot hike that takes you to the ridge above the Gemstone Bowls that sit above the Blackcomb Glacier. To access Spanky's Ladder, get off the top of the Glacier Express Chairlift, turn left, and follow the traverse leading off to the right side (looking downhill). At the end of the traverse is a narrow (one-person wide) boot hike that takes you to the top of the ridge above the Gemstone Bowls.

> **NOTE**: This is expert skiing territory with very steep Double-Black and Triple-Black runs in the Gemstone Bowls!

Secret Bowl

To access Secret Bowl and the runs that lead down from it, you need to take the 7th Heaven Express Chairlift up, start down Blue Line (Blue), and then traverse left (looking downhill) over into Secret Bowl. Secret Bowl sits above the Saudan Couloir, the Jersey Cream Express Chairlift area, and the Glacier Express Chairlift area.

Secret Bowl seen from Horstman Hut. The entrance to Saudan Couloir is on the left, Secret Bowl is in the middle, and Blue Line leads down into the Glacier Express Chairlift area on the front right. (Source: Nick Jones)

Looking up at Cougar Chutes and the end of Secret Bowl from the Rendezvous Lodge area on a bluebird day. (Source: Nick Jones)

◆◆ **Cougar Chutes:** Cougar Chutes is a steep Double-Black run that starts at the very end of Secret Bowl and runs down into the Jersey Cream Express Chairlift area below. The entrance to Cougar Chutes is narrow and steep but then it turns into a wide, steep run with small trees. To access this run, you need to take the 7th Heaven Express Chairlift up and access Secret Bowl.

> **NOTE**: This is a steep run with many small trees. It is important to keep control of your skiing to avoid falling, sliding down the run, and hitting the trees on the way down.

◆ **Clean Out:** Clean Out is a short, steep Black chute entrance into the side of Secret Bowl Run (Black). It starts at the top from Secret Bowl and ends on Secret Bowl Run.

> **NOTE**: This run should only be approached when there is sufficient snow.

◆◆ **Pakalolo:** Pakalolo is a steep, bumpy Double-Black run that starts with a chute just below Secret Bowl and turns into a steep mogul field that leads down to Blue Line (Blue).

> **NOTE**: This is a steep, challenging run (similar to the others runs along this face below Secret Bowl) and should be approached with caution.

♦♦ **Pipeline:** Pipeline is a steep, narrow, rocky Double-Black chute (located halfway between Secret Bowl run and Pakalolo) that curves down under a cliff to end on the mogul field below Pakalolo (Double Black).

> **NOTE**: This is a steep, challenging run and should be approached with caution.

♦♦♦**Purple Haze:** Purple Haze is a steep, narrow, rocky, difficult Triple-Black run that starts over a cornice, becomes a bench, and then runs down onto the mogul field below Cougar Chutes (Black) and above Coyote Road (Blue). You can access it by entering Cougar Chutes, traversing to the left, and then entering the run over the top of a cornice.

> **NOTE**: This is one of the most challenging runs on Blackcomb given how narrow, steep, and exposed it is. This run should only be approached if you have expert skills and when there is sufficient snow.

Secret Bowl between Saudan Couloir and the Glacier Express Chairlift area.
(Source: FATMAP.com)

♦ **Secret Bowl Run:** Secret Bowl run is a steep, wide Black mogul run that comes out of Secret Bowl through an opening in the cliff face and then runs down to Blue Line (Blue) below. This is the easiest Black run out of Secret Bowl.

♦ **Swiss Cheese:** Swiss Cheese is a steep Black run that zigzags down the face below Secret Bowl and ends on Blue Line (Blue).

NOTE: Similar to Clean Out, this run should only be approached when there is sufficient snow to provide a skiable surface.

♦♦ **The Curl/Lone Pine:** The Curl/Lone Pine is a steep, narrow, Double-Black run that starts on the side of Secret Bowl and runs down a bench underneath a cliff to Blue Line (Blue) below. This run is known for the one small pine tree that grows near the bottom of it.

NOTE: This is a steep, challenging run with lots of exposure. It should be approached with caution and only when there is sufficient snow to provide a skiable surface.

A group of skiers with a wonderful sun halo and sundogs at the top of the Glacier Express Chairlift on a frosty winter day. (Source: Jan Ludvik)

Blackcomb Glacier Area

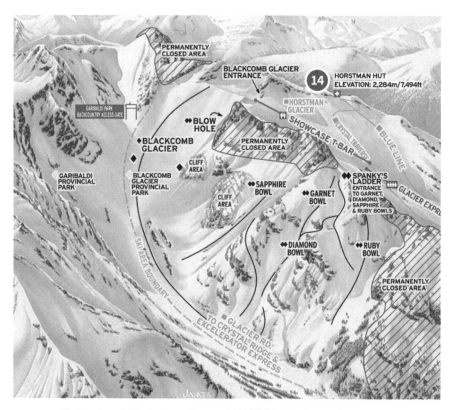

The Blackcomb Glacier area. (Source: 2022/23 Whistler Blackcomb Trail Map)

Skiing the Blackcomb Glacier is an amazing experience when weather and snow conditions are good. The Blackcomb Glacier is located on the other side of the ridge to the northeast of the Glacier Express Chairlift area. You can access it via a boot hike over the ridge starting from the top of the Showcase T-bar at the top of the Glacier Express Chairlift area.

The Blackcomb Glacier is in a large, wide alpine bowl that leads down to Blackcomb Glacier Road (a Blue run that takes you out and back down towards the bottom of the Crystal Ridge Express Chairlift). As you ski out at the bottom of the Blackcomb Glacier, you can look up to the left and see the expert Gemstone Bowls—Sapphire Bowl, Diamond Bowl, and Ruby Bowl.

The Blackcomb Glacier area offers amazing open alpine, off-piste skiing for strong intermediate and expert skiers, with runs ranging from the main Blue down the middle of the glacier to Black and Double-Black runs on the sides.

There used to be a well-known ice cave in the lower half of the Blackcomb Glacier, however this was covered up by an avalanche in the 2022/23 ski season. At this time, it is unclear if the ice cave will reappear in the coming seasons.

> **NOTE:** All of Blackcomb Glacier is open alpine, so it can be very challenging if visibility and/or snow conditions are poor. The glacier and the bowls found here are ungroomed/off-piste skiing. Only attempt this area if you are comfortable with this type of skiing and snow and weather conditions are good.

Locals' Tips

- Ask around about conditions in Blackcomb Glacier before you go. Although it can be amazing with good snow and visibility, it can be unpleasant with poor visibility and hard, crusty, difficult snow conditions.
- Take your time going up the boot hike into Blackcomb Glacier, as it is steep and can get icy with heavy use.
- At the top of the boot hike into the glacier, take a moment to look down at the Blow Hole. This is a unique wind-sculpted feature on the left side (looking downhill) of this area.

Gondolas/Lifts

There are no gondolas or lifts in the Blackcomb Glacier area. Access to Blackcomb Glacier is via a boot hike from the top of the Showcase T-Bar over the ridge into the Blackcomb Glacier area.

Lodges/Huts

There are no lodges or huts in the Blackcomb Glacier area.

Main Routes

There are no Green runs in the Blackcomb Glacier area.

■ **Blackcomb Glacier:** The Blackcomb Glacier run is the main Blue run that goes down the middle of this area and then ends on the Blackcomb Glacier Road (a Blue run that leads down to the bottom of the Crystal Ridge Express Chairlift).

There is no main Black route down into the Blackcomb Glacier area.

Blue Runs

■ **Blackcomb Glacier:** The Blackcomb Glacier is a large, wide Blue run down the middle of the bowl. You can access the top of the glacier via the Showcase T-Bar followed by a boot hike up over the ridge into the Blackcomb Glacier area. Starting at the top of the ridge, traverse across the top of the Blackcomb Glacier to the middle, ski down the middle of the glacier, and then continue to Blackcomb Glacier Road (Blue).

NOTE: Although this can be a fun, challenging Blue run with good snow and good visibility, with poor snow and visibility, it is more like a Black. Either way, skiing this bowl requires good off-piste skiing skills.

Looking down from Ruby Bowl at skiers on Blackcomb Glacier Road coming out of the bottom of the Blackcomb Glacier area. (Source: Jennifer Nairn)

■ **Blackcomb Glacier Road:** Blackcomb Glacier Road is the long, narrow Blue run that comes out of the bottom of the Blackcomb Glacier, passes the bottom of the Crystal Ridge Express Chairlift, and continues to the bottom of the Excelerator Express Chairlift.

Black Runs/Areas

The Black runs of the Gemstone Bowls on the side of the Blackcomb Glacier.
(Source: FATMAP.com)

◆ **Blow Hole:** The Blowhole is the famous Black feature on the left side (looking downhill) of the Blackcomb Glacier. It gets its unique half-pipe-like shape from the winds that howl over the ridge and down into this area. Access at the top of the Blow Hole is near the entrance into the Blackcomb Glacier area. At the bottom, you exit into the bottom of the Blackcomb Glacier bowl.

♦♦ **Surf's Up:** Surf's Up is a narrow, steep Double-Black chute accessible from the left side (looking downhill) of Winky Pop (Black). At the bottom of this chute, you can join up with Winky Pop again and exit into the bottom of the Blackcomb Glacier bowl.

♦ **Wind Lip:** The Wind Lip is a very large snow ridge generated by the wind coming over the ridge from the 7th Heaven area into the Blackcomb Glacier area. Below the lip is an ungroomed Black area that leads down the right side (looking downhill) of the glacier and ends in the bottom of the bowl.

♦ **Winky Pop:** Winky Pop is a Black run that goes over a rock ledge below its smaller but more difficult sibling, Surf's Up (Double Black). It is accessible by traversing to the left (looking downhill) below the Blow Hole (Black).

Heading up the boot hike to the entrance into the Blackcomb Glacier on a frosty day.
(Source: Jennifer Nairn)

Gemstone Bowls Area

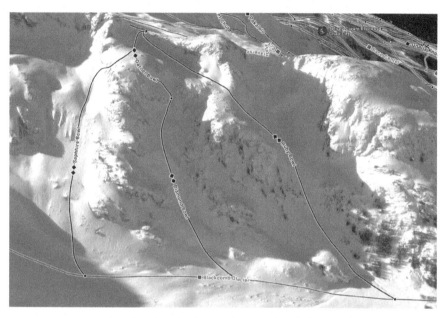

The Gemstone Bowls area above Blackcomb Glacier.
(Source: FATMAP.com)

The Gemstone Bowls are a group of bowls high up on the left side (looking downhill) of the Blackcomb Glacier area. These bowls are accessible from the Glacier Express Chairlift area via Spanky's Ladder. The Gemstone Bowls area gets its name because of the names of the bowls in this area: Diamond Bowl, Garnet Bowl, Ruby Bowl, and Sapphire Bowl.

Similar to the Whistler Peak area and Saudan Couloir, the Gemstone Bowls offer challenging, steep, open alpine skiing for expert skiers. The Gemstone Bowls are known for their Black and Double-Black runs, amazing scenery, and deep powder that collects in this area after winter storms.

> **NOTE**: All the Gemstone Bowls are expert skiing zones that require strong off-piste and steep skiing skills. Only approach these bowls when snow and weather conditions are good.

Gondolas/Lifts

There are no gondolas or lifts in the Gemstone Bowls area. Access to the Gemstone Bowl area is via the Glacier Express Chairlift and then Spanky's Ladder.

Spanky's Ladder: Spanky's Ladder is the access path to get into the Gemstone Bowls. You can access Spanky's Ladder by following Spanky's Ladder Traverse, which starts near the top of the Glacier Express Chairlift. At the end of the traverse, there is a narrow (one-person wide) and steep boot hike—Spanky's Ladder—that takes you to the top of the ridge above the Gemstone Bowls.

Lodges/Huts

There are no lodges or huts in the Gemstone Bowl area.

Locals' Tips

- Ask around about conditions in Gemstone Bowls before you go. Although it can be amazing with good snow and visibility, it can be unpleasant with poor visibility and hard, crusty, difficult snow conditions.
- If you are going to Spanky's Ladder and the Gemstone Bowls for the first time, find someone who knows this area to help guide you through the complex entrances into the various chutes and bowls.
- Take your time going up Spanky's Ladder, it is a steep boot hike and can get icy with heavy use.

Main Routes

There are no Green or Blue runs in the Gemstone Bowl area.

There is no main Black route through the Gemstone Bowls. Each of the bowls is a viable route down to the Blackcomb Glacier bowl. The easiest Black route through this area is through Garnet Bowl and down into Ruby Bowl.

Skiers and boarders boot hiking up Spanky's Ladder to get to the Gemstone Bowls.
(Source: Cristin Flynn)

Garnet Bowl

Garnet Bowl is the small Black bowl immediately below the top of Spanky's Ladder. There are different routes/traverses through, around, and above Garnet Bowl that lead to the other Gemstone Bowls.

Diamond Bowl

Diamond Bowl is the middle bowl of the three main Gemstone bowls. It sits directly below Garnet Bowl and is known for its challenging chute entrances, such as Wild Thing (Double Black) and the Diamond Bowl Left Entrance (Double Black).

◆◆ **Calvin:** Calvin is a short Double-Black run below the Diamond Bowl Left Entrance (Double Black). You can access the top of Calvin by traversing and climbing up from the left side (looking downhill) of the Diamond Bowl Left Entrance. Calvin ends at the top of Hobbes (Double Black).

NOTE: This run should only be attempted when there is sufficient snow depth to allow for safe skiing.

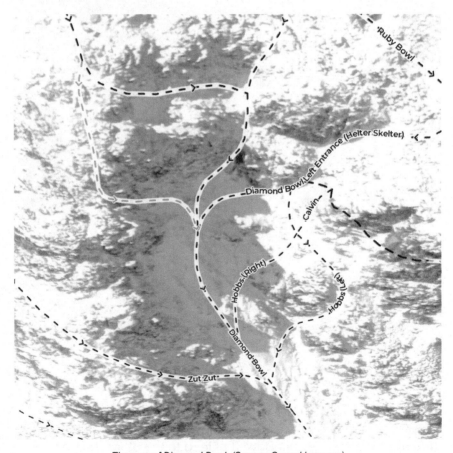

The runs of Diamond Bowl. (Source: Openskimap.org)

◆◆ Diamond Bowl: Diamond Bowl is a steep, bumpy, ungroomed alpine bowl that leads down to Blackcomb Glacier Road (Blue). It is accessible via several Double-Black entrances down the cliff between Diamond Bowl and Garnet Bowl above.

 NOTE: This bowl along with the other Gemstone Bowls are all expert skiing zones with steep, bumpy, rocky sections and chutes.

◆◆ Diamond Bowl Main Entrance: The Diamond Bowl Main Entrance is the central entrance down from Garnet Bowl into the Diamond Bowl below. There are two access routes from Spanky's Ladder through the Garnet Bowl to the top of the main Diamond Bowl Main Entrance: one goes to the right (looking downhill), and the other goes to the left (looking downhill) of the short cliff in the middle bottom of Garnet Bowl.

 NOTE: This entrance is a steep, rocky chute. Approach with caution.

The Double-Black Diamond Bowl entrances. (Source: Cristin Flynn)

◆◆ **Diamond Bowl Left Entrance:** The Diamond Bowl Left Entrance (also called Helter Skelter) is a more challenging entrance into Diamond Bowl. You can access this entrance by continuing further to the left in Garnet Bowl (heading towards Ruby Bowl) and then curving right down towards Diamond Bowl. This entrance is a narrow chute above the large cliff on the left side (looking downhill) of Diamond Bowl.

NOTE: This is a narrow, rocky, very difficult entrance and should only be attempted when there is sufficient snow.

◆◆ **Hobbes:** Hobbes is actually two separate rocky Double-Black chutes that go down through a lower cliff face on the left side (looking downhill) of Diamond Bowl. You can access these chutes by traversing to the left of the Diamond Bowl Left Entrance into Diamond Bowl.

NOTE: Both the entrance and these two chutes are expert skiing territory that should only be attempted when there is sufficient snow depth to provide safe skiing. Ideally ski with someone who knows the area and can guide the way.

◆◆ **Wild Thing:** Wild Thing is a steep Double-Black chute entrance down the cliffs on the right side (looking downhill) of Diamond Bowl. You can access this route by skiing to the right into Garnet Bowl and then curving left to the cliffs above the right side of Diamond Bowl.

NOTE: This is a narrow, rocky, very difficult entrance and should only be attempted when there is sufficient snow.

Ruby Bowl

Ruby Bowl is the furthest to the left (looking downhill) of the Gemstone Bowls. The Spanky's Shoulder Route (Double Black) is considered to be the easiest route into the Ruby Bowl area (but is still a challenging Double Black).

◆◆◆ **Bad Attitude:** Bad Attitude is an extremely difficult, Triple-Black chute (with a very fitting name) that leads down to a sloping bench between big cliffs above and below. The start of this run is accessible via a very difficult, rocky traverse from the top of Calvin (Double Black) in the Diamond Bowl. Bad Attitude exits into the lower end of Ruby Bowl (Double Black).

NOTE: This is a very difficult, challenging run accessed via a difficult, rocky traverse. This run should only be attempted when there is sufficient snow.

◆◆ **Midway Rock:** Midway Rock is a steep Double-Black route down the left side (looking downhill) of upper Ruby Bowl. It is named after the Midway Rock cliff face that runs across the upper middle of Ruby Bowl. This run is accessible via a long traverse along the ridge to the left of the top of Spanky's Ladder, down Spanky's Chute (Double Black), and then across the traverse that runs along the top of Ruby Bowl. Midway runs down and exits onto the bottom of Ruby Bowl, which then leads to Blackcomb Glacier Road (Blue).

NOTE: This is an expert skiing zone with steep, bumpy, rocky sections and chutes.

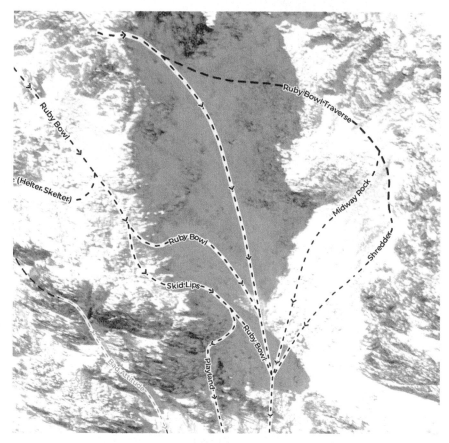

The runs of Ruby Bowl. (Source: Openskimap.org)

◆◆ **Playland:** Playland is a tight, steep Double-Black gully that runs below a cliff along the right side (looking downhill) of Ruby Bowl. You can access Playland by going right below the cliffs at the bottom of Skid Lips (Double Black). Playland exits into the bottom of Ruby Bowl.

> **NOTE**: This is a steep, tight gully between rock outcrops and cliff faces.

Ruby Bowl with the top of Shredder just below the cliffs behind the skier. (Source: Jennifer Nairn)

◆◆ **Ruby Bowl:** Ruby Bowl is a big, steep, bumpy Double-Black bowl. There are two routes to access Ruby Bowl. The upper and more difficult route follows a traverse to the left of Spanky's Ladder across to Spanky's Chute (Double Black) and down into Ruby Bowl. The lower and easier route is down and left into Garnet Bowl, over to Spanky's Shoulder, and then down into Ruby Bowl. The exit out of the bottom of Ruby Bowl is onto Blackcomb Glacier Road (Blue), which takes you to the bottom of the Crystal Ridge Express Chairlift.

◆◆ **Shredder:** Shredder is a steep Double-Black run that is the leftmost route (looking downhill) down Ruby Bowl. This run is accessible via a long traverse along the ridge to the left of the top of

Spanky's Ladder, down Spanky's Chute (Double Black), and across the traverse along the top of Ruby Bowl.

> **NOTE**: Shredder runs down the side of Ruby Bowl below a large, out-of-bounds cliff area. Don't stray into the out-of-bounds area, as you will be at risk of losing your pass if you are caught by the ski patrol.

◆◆ **Skid Lips:** Skid Lips is a steep Double-Black run along the shoulder of a cliff along the right side (looking downhill) of Ruby Bowl, parallel to Spanky's Shoulder (Double Black). You can access the top of Skid Lips from the right side (looking downhill) of Spanky's Shoulder (Double Black), and it exits into the middle of Ruby Bowl.

> **NOTE**: Don't stray too far to the right on this run, as there is a steep, rocky cliff along the right side (looking downhill).

◆◆ **Spanky's Chute:** Spanky's Chute is a challenging, steep, Double-Black chute that leads into the top of Ruby Bowl. The top of Spanky's Chute is accessible via a long traverse along the ridge that runs above Garnet Bowl. Access to the traverse starts to the left of the top of Spanky's Ladder.

> **NOTE**: This is a steep, narrow, rocky chute that requires significant control and expertise to navigate.

◆◆ **Spanky's Shoulder:** Spanky's Shoulder is the easiest route into Ruby Bowl but is still an expert Double-Black run. You can access Spanky's Shoulder by dropping into Garnet Bowl below Spanky's Ladder and then skiing to the left (looking downhill) through Garnet Bowl. This leads to the top of Spanky's Shoulder, which runs down into the right side (looking downhill) of Ruby Bowl.

Sapphire Bowl

Sapphire Bowl is considered to be the most challenging of the Gemstone Bowls. It is a steep, bumpy, rocky Double-Black bowl with difficult chute entrances and exits.

◆◆ **Family Jewels:** Family Jewels is a steep Double-Black run down the left side (looking downhill) of Sapphire Bowl. It starts at the bottom of the Sapphire Bowl Entrances, runs parallel to the Sapphire Chutes (Double Black), and then curves left onto a bench that cuts across to the lower end of Diamond Bowl. It exits onto the Blackcomb Glacier (Blue).

Looking down into Garnet Bowl towards the Ruby Bowl entrance on a fresh snow day.
(Source: Anna Lana)

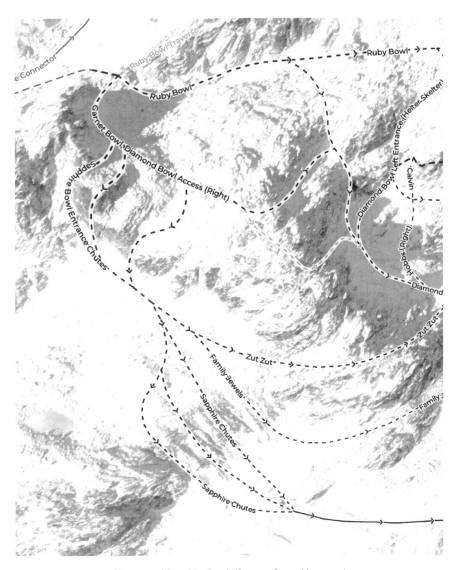

The runs of Sapphire Bowl. (Source: Openskimap.org)

◆◆ **Sapphire Bowl Entrances:** The Sapphire Bowl Entrances are a series of Double-Black chute entrances from Garnet Bowl at the top down into Sapphire Bowl below. You can access these entrances from the right side (looking downhill) of the traverse that runs along the right side (looking downhill) of Garnet Bowl. The easiest of the entrances into Sapphire Bowl is the lowest one along the Garnet Bowl traverse.

NOTE: Access to the top of Sapphire Bowl Entrances is a very challenging route through rocks and along a cliff. The entrances into Sapphire Bowl are steep, rocky, challenging chutes that should be approached with caution and respect.

◆◆ Sapphire Chutes: The Sapphire Chutes are three very difficult, Double-Black chutes along the bottom edge of Sapphire Bowl. They exit down onto Blackcomb Glacier (Blue).

NOTE: Only approach these chutes when there is good snow and visibility.

◆◆ Zut Zut: Zut Zut is a challenging Double-Black run that starts from the left side of Family Jewels (Double Black), curves down to the left (looking downhill), and runs diagonally down across a bench between cliffs above and below. It runs over to and ends in the bottom end of Diamond Bowl (Double Black). This run has a reputation for often having deep snow due to its protected location under a large cliff.

NOTE: When going down this run, do not stray to the right (looking downhill), as there is a steep cliff below the run on this side.

7th Heaven Express Chairlift Area

The 7th Heaven area on Blackcomb.
(Source: 2022/23 Whistler Blackcomb Trail Map)

The 7th Heaven Express Chairlift area is a wonderful open alpine ski area on the southeastern side of Blackcomb. This is a great area for intermediate and advanced skiers and boarders.

7th Heaven is known for its long big Blue runs—Panorama, Cloud Nine, and Hugh's Heaven. In between these runs you'll find plenty of open alpine off-piste skiing and glade skiing below the tree line. There are also many Black run options, including:

- Everglades (wonderful glade skiing)
- Angel Dust and Sunburn (bumps)

- Xhiggy's Meadow (open alpine, bumps)
- Lakeside Bowl (open alpine, bumps)

You can access the bottom of the 7th Heaven Express Chairlift via two long, narrow Green runs: 7th Avenue (from the top of the Jersey Cream Express Chairlift) and Expressway (from the Rendezvous Lodge area).

The 7th Heaven Express Chairlift also provides access to:

- Saudan Couloir area
- Secret Bowl area
- Glacier Express Chairlift area

To exit the 7th Heaven area, take either Sunset Boulevard (Green) out from below the bottom of the chairlift or follow Green Line (Green) out from the top. You can also take Blue Line (Blue) over the ridge behind Horstman Hut to exit into the Glacier Express Chairlift area.

> **NOTE:** A large part of the 7th Heaven area is in the open alpine, so it can be very challenging if visibility and/or snow conditions are poor. The 7th Heaven Express Chairlift also gets very busy on good snow/weather days and on weekends.

Locals' Tips

- The Black glade runs below 7th Avenue, Expressway, and Last Resort are in an area of Blackcomb that is not used heavily and can offer fun, challenging expert glade skiing.
- On a new snow/powder day, 7th Heaven is a go-to area for locals looking for long, amazing fresh tracks in the pow! On such days, head over to this area early to get in some fresh tracks before it gets too crowded.
- If you like glade skiing, the Everglades (Black) area below Green Line (Green) is wonderful when there is good snow and visibility. This is one of my favorite glade skiing areas in the resort.
- As the weather warms, 7th Heaven is prone to thaw/freeze cycles and can become icy—the frozen, chopped snow and ice bombs on the 7th Heaven runs are legendary. On days like these, give it some time to soften up before you head over.

Gondolas/Lifts

7th Heaven Express Chairlift: This is the four-person, high-speed chairlift that services this area of Blackcomb Mountain.

Heading up the 7th Heaven Express Chairlift with the Garbanzo runs of Whistler in the background. (Source: Alice Green)

Lodges/Huts

Horstman Hut: Horstman Hut is a small hut at the top of the 7th Heaven Express Chairlift. It offers limited food, snack, and drink options and has a small indoor sitting area. On a nice day, the deck at Horstman Hut offers one of the most beautiful views in all of Whistler Blackcomb. There are also washrooms in a small building next to the hut.

Main Routes

There is no main Green route from the top to the bottom of the 7th Heaven area.

■ **Cloud Nine, Hugh's Heaven,** or **Panorama:** These three wide, steep Blues all run down from the top to the bottom of the 7th Heaven area.

There is no single Black route from the top to the bottom of the 7th Heaven area.

Green Runs

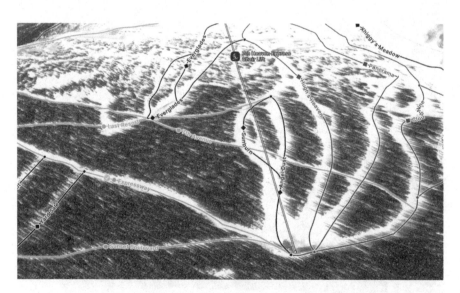

The lower Green runs in the 7th Heaven Express Chairlift area.
(Source: FATMAP.com)

● **7th Avenue:** 7th Avenue is a long, narrow, relatively flat Green run that starts near the top of the Jersey Cream Express Chairlift, runs around the side of the mountain, cutting across Hugh's Heaven (Blue) and Panorama (Blue), and ending on Cloud Nine (Blue). You can take any one of these Blue runs down to the bottom of the 7th Heaven Express Chairlift.

NOTE: Several other runs cut across 7th Avenue, so watch out for other skiers and be ready to avoid a collision if necessary.

Heading down 7th Avenue towards the bottom of the 7th Heaven area.
(Source: Susan Rogers)

A group of skiers and boarders enjoying the open alpine of 7th Heaven on a spring day.
(Source: Nick Jones)

● **Expressway:** Expressway is a long, narrow, relatively flat Green run from near the top of the Catskinner Express Chairlift/ Rendezvous Lodge area, around the side of the mountain, and down to the bottom of the 7th Heaven Express Chairlift. This is the lower route into the 7th Heaven area.

● **Upper Green Line:** Upper Green Line is the Green run that zigzags down from the top of the 7th Heaven Express Chairlift and exits to the right (looking downhill) towards the top of the Jersey Cream Express Chairlift and the Rendezvous Lodge area. Initially this run is narrow and has a couple of steep spots, but it widens out as it exits out of the 7th Heaven area.

> **NOTE**: Although this is a Green run, it has some challenging spots, can have heavy traffic, and is exposed in the open alpine at the top of 7th Heaven. Depending on the conditions, this run should be considered a dark Green verging on Blue.

● **Last Resort:** Last Resort is a long, narrow Green run that cuts diagonally across the lower right (looking downhill) of the 7th Heaven area. It provides an exit above Angel Dust (Black) and Sunburn (Black) in case you decide that these two mogul runs are not for you. You can take Last Resort down to Expressway (Green) and return to the 7th Heaven area, or follow Last Resort out of the

7th Heaven area down to the bottom of the Catskinner Express Chairlift.

● **Sunset Boulevard:** Sunset Boulevard (Green) is a very long, narrow Green run from the bottom of the 7th Heaven Express Chairlift down around the mountain, and ending on Easy Out (Green). Easy Out then runs down to the Blackcomb Gondola Mid Station.

NOTE: Given its southwestern (sun-facing) orientation on the mountain and the traffic down this run, it can become icy as the day progresses. It can also be quite busy, as skiers use it to exit the 7th Heaven area.

Blue Runs

■ **Cloud Nine:** Cloud Nine is one of the three wide, steep Blue runs down through the 7th Heaven area. Cloud Nine starts at the first bend in Upper Green Line (Green) where it comes down from the top of the 7th Heaven Express Chairlift. The top part of Cloud Nine runs across the top of the 7th Heaven area for a short stretch and then drops down through the open alpine with areas of ungroomed, off-piste snow on either side. You can find glade-skiing opportunities on either side of the run where it starts to enter the tree line. Cloud Nine ends down at the bottom of the 7th Heaven Express Chairlift.

NOTE: Compared to other hills, the 7th Heaven Blues are large and steep, so approach with caution. Given its southwestern (sun-facing) orientation on the mountain and the traffic down this run, it can become bumpy and icy as the day progresses.

■ **Hugh's Heaven:** Hugh's Heaven is very similar to Cloud Nine (Blue) and is another wide, steep, groomed Blue run down through the 7th Heaven area. Hugh's Heaven starts at the first bend in Upper Green Line (Green), runs parallel to Cloud Nine, and ends at the bottom of the 7th Heaven Express Chairlift. It offers opportunities for open alpine off-piste skiing as well as glade skiing on either side of the run. The run is named after Hugh Smythe, one of the founding fathers of Whistler Blackcomb. This run was one of his favorite runs on Blackcomb.

NOTE: Similar to Cloud Nine, this is a long, steep Blue that can become bumpy and icy with use and due to thaw/freeze cycles.

The big, wide Blue runs—Cloud Nine, Hugh's Heaven, and Panorama—of the 7th Heaven Express Chairlift area. (Source: FATMAP.com)

HISTORY NOTES

Hugh Smythe

Hugh Smythe, a well-known figure in the world of skiing and mountain-resort development, first arrived in Whistler in the late 1960s as a ski patroller. His passion and determination would soon lead him to play an instrumental role in the development of both Whistler and Blackcomb Mountains. Smythe's keen vision and hard work helped transform the mountains into world-class ski resorts through pioneering innovations such as high-speed lifts and integrated resort infrastructure. As one of the driving forces behind the merger of Whistler and Blackcomb in 1997, Hugh was also instrumental in establishing Whistler Blackcomb as the largest and most popular ski destination in North America.

Source: *Ski Canada Magazine* https://skicanadamag.com/blackcomb-40/

■ **Panorama:** Panorama is the third big, wide Blue run on 7th Heaven. It starts a bit further down the hill at the second bend of Green Line (Green), curves under the 7th Heaven Express Chairlift, and cuts back across the hill, crossing Hugh's Heaven (Blue). Panorama then runs down between Cloud Nine and Hugh's Heaven to end at the bottom of the 7th Heaven Express Chairlift.

NOTE: This is a long, steep Blue that can become bumpy and icy with use and due to thaw/freeze cycles. The top of this run can be quite busy, as it is one of the routes that skiers use to exit out of the 7th Heaven area.

■ **Sluiceway:** Sluiceway is a short, ungroomed Blue run that starts on the side of Cloud Nine (Blue) and exits back onto Cloud Nine further downhill. It gets its name from the fact that it runs over a creek that runs from the lake above down to Fitzsimmons Creek below. This run is not groomed and can become quite bumpy with use.

Black Runs/Areas

◆ **Angel Dust:** Angel Dust is a Black mogul run that starts at the same point as Sunburn (Black) and then runs parallel to it. Access to this run is from the right side (looking downhill) of Hugh's Heaven (Blue). Angel Dust then crosses 7th Avenue (Green), and then continues down to the bottom of the 7th Heaven Express Chairlift. On a fresh powder day, this run offers some amazing, fluffy bump skiing.

NOTE: Angel Dust can become icy with use and due to thaw/ freeze cycles.

◆ **Everglades:** The Everglades is a wide area of Black glade skiing that runs from Upper Green Line (Green) above down to Last Resort (Green) and 7th Avenue (Green) below. The upper section of the Everglades includes smaller trees and open areas, while there are steeper, tighter glades on the lower section. On a sunny, fresh snow day, this is one of my favorite areas to ski on Blackcomb!

NOTE: This is an expert glade-skiing zone. Watch for tree wells, drops, and other terrain challenges in this glade area.

♦ **Lakeside Bowl:** Lakeside Bowl is a large, ungroomed Black alpine bowl on the left side (looking downhill) of the 7th Heaven area. You can access it by following the Lakeside Bowl Traverse that starts at the top of Cloud Nine (Blue) and continuing along the traverse under the cliffs to the top of the Lakeside Bowl area. There are a variety of routes that lead down into the bowl, which then exit out onto Cloud Nine below.

> **NOTE**: The Lakeside Bowl Traverse is quite challenging and steep in parts. The bottom of the bowl can also be quite flat, so either be prepared to pole or pick a route that will give you enough speed to ski or ride out of the bowl.

The Black runs on the west side of the 7th Heaven Express Chairlift area. (Source: FATMAP.com)

♦ **Raptor's Ride:** Raptor's Ride is the longest of the four bumpy Black glade runs that start on Expressway (Green) and lead down to Sunset Boulevard (Green). The trees on this run are well spaced, and with fresh snow this can be a wonderful, fluffy bump glade run!

> **NOTE**: Without snow, or with heavy use, the bumps/moguls in this run can become quite large and challenging. Scope out this run from the top before committing to go down it.

◆ **Sunburn:** Sunburn is a Black mogul run and is the sibling of Angel Dust (Black). Access to the top of Sunburn and Angel Dust (which start at the same point) is from the right side (looking downhill) of Hugh's Heaven (Blue). This run crosses 7th Avenue (Green), and then continues down to the bottom of the 7th Heaven Express Chairlift. On a fresh powder day, this is a locals' favorite for fluffy bumps!

NOTE: Similar to the other runs on 7th Heaven, Sunburn can become icy with use and due to thaw/freeze cycles.

◆ **Watch Out:** Watch Out is similar to Raptor's Ride (Black) and is another bumpy Black glade run that starts on Expressway (Green) and leads down to Sunset Boulevard (Green).

NOTE: With heavy snowfall and use, the bumps/moguls in this run can become quite large and challenging.

◆ **Where's Joe:** Where's Joe is a shorter, bumpy black glade that starts on Expressway (Green) and leads down to Sunset Boulevard (Green).

◆ **Yard Sale:** Yard Sale is the final and shortest of the four bumpy Black glade runs that start on Expressway (Green) and lead down to Sunset Boulevard (Green).

◆ **Xhiggy's Meadow:** Xhiggy's Meadow is a steep, bumpy Black slope just below the start of the Lakeside Bowl Traverse and to the left of Cloud Nine (Blue). The exit out of the bottom of Xhiggy's is onto Cloud Nine.

NOTE: Xhiggy's starts in the alpine zone but ends in the beginning of the tree line. As a result, there are often small trees poking up through the snow on the lower end of this area. Watch for and avoid these 'ski grabbers'.

Other Areas

Unmarked Open Alpine and Glades: The 7th Heaven area provides a wide range of unmarked open alpine and glade-skiing options between the marked runs. On a new snow day, the 7th Heaven area is a locals' favorite go-to area on Blackcomb for fresh tracks and great skiing.

NOTE: When skiing in these unmarked areas, watch for and avoid unexpected drops, tree wells, creeks, and other hazards.

♦ **7th Heaven Avenue Glades:** The 7th Heaven Avenue Glades is an area of unmarked, tight, Black glades that run from 7th Heaven Avenue (Green) down to Expressway (Green) or to Easy Out (Green).

NOTE: This is an expert glade-skiing zone with tight trees, drops, and other terrain challenges. Approach with caution!

The 7th Heaven Express area with Black Tusk in the background.
(Source: Marc Gault)

Saudan Couloir Area

The Saudan Couloir area on Blackcomb.
(Source: FATMAP.com)

T he Saudan Couloir is a large, steep couloir located above the Jersey Cream Bowl and below Chainsaw Ridge in the high alpine zone of Blackcomb Mountain.

This area is famous for the Double-Black Saudan Couloir run that goes down the middle of the couloir as well as for the other Black/ Double-Black/Triple-Black runs on either side of it. It is also known for the Couloir Extreme Race that is run here. The name of this area comes from Sylvain Saudan, who spent many years skiing in

British Columbia and is considered by many to be the 'godfather' of extreme skiing.

Access to the Saudan Couloir is via the 7th Heaven Express Chairlift. To access the couloir, ski to the left at the top of the chairlift, continue below Horstman Hut, start going down Blue Line (Blue), and then traverse to the left (looking downhill) to the Saudan Couloir or Quasar (Black) entrances.

The Saudan Couloir and its associated Black, Double-Black, and Triple-Black runs are favorites among local and visiting expert, freeride skiers who want to test their skills on this area of Blackcomb Mountain.

NOTE: Similar to the other high alpine areas on Whistler Blackcomb, this area can be difficult and even dangerous if visibility and/or snow conditions are poor. The 7th Heaven Express Chairlift—which provides access to this area—also gets very busy on good snow/weather days and on weekends.

Locals' Tips

- Consider skiing the Saudan Couloir and related runs on days when there is good snow. The runs in this area are challenging enough without them being icy or bare of snow.
- The cornice below Chainsaw Ridge and above the couloir is controlled regularly by the ski patrol, however, it always presents a risk. Do not approach the edge of the cornice unless you are following an entry route into the couloir.
- Given that the cornice is regularly blasted by the ski patrol, there is often a significant amount of debris in the couloir below the cornice. Watch for and avoid this debris as you ski down into the couloir.
- Most of the slopes on either side of the couloir are in the pitch range that makes them highly susceptible to avalanches. Ski with caution and practice safe skiing to avoid triggering and getting caught in an avalanche.

Gondolas/Lifts

7th Heaven Express Chairlift: This is the four-person, high-speed chairlift that provides access to the 7th Heaven area as well as the Saudan Couloir area.

Lodges/Huts

Horstman Hut: Horstman Hut is a small hut at the top of the 7th Heaven Express Chairlift. It offers limited food, snack, and drink options and has a small indoor sitting area. On a nice day, the deck at Horstman Hut offers one of the most beautiful views in all of Whistler Blackcomb. There are also washrooms in a small building next to the hut.

The amazing view from the Horstman Hut deck towards Whistler and the valley on a beautiful spring day. (Source: Nick Jones)

Main Routes

There are no main Green or Blue routes in this area.

◆◆ **Saudan Couloir:** The Saudan Couloir is the main Double-Black run down the middle of the couloir. It starts at the top of the couloir and runs down into the Jersey Cream Chairlift area.

Green and Blue Runs

There are no Green or Blue runs in the Saudan Couloir area.

Black Runs/Areas

The upper Black runs on the south side of the Saudan Couloir including Whiplash, Bushwip, Bushrat, Hawaii 5-0, and False Face. (Source: Openskimap.org)

♦♦♦ **Bushrat:** Bushrat is a steep, challenging Triple-Black chute into the Saudan Couloir between Hawaii 5-0 (Triple Black) and Bushwip (Triple Black). The entrance into this chute is from Chainsaw Ridge (Black) and then over the cornice. Below the cornice, Bushrat runs diagonally down into the couloir below.

> **NOTE**: The entrance into this run over the cornice is very difficult and can be dangerous depending on conditions. If in doubt, take a pass on this one. Approach only with extreme caution and ideally with a local guide!

♦♦♦ **Bushwip:** Bushwip is a short Triple-Black chute into the Saudan Couloir below. The entrance into this run is from Chainsaw Ridge (Black), over a cornice, and down into a steep, rocky chute. Bushwhip ends on Bushrat.

> **NOTE**: The entrance into this run over the cornice is very difficult, rocky, and dangerous depending on conditions. If in doubt, take a pass on this one.

♦♦♦ Bushrat Shoulder: Bushrat Shoulder is steep, challenging Triple-Black run parallel to and just below Bushrat (Triple Black). The entrance to this run is from the right side (looking downhill) of Bushrat. It then runs along a bench between the cliffs below Bushrat.

> **NOTE**: Similar to Bushrat and the other Triple Blacks on this side of the Couloir, approach this run with caution and only where there is sufficient snow cover to make it skiable. There is a steep cliff on the right side (looking downhill) of this run, so stay to the left.

♦ Chainsaw Ridge: Chainsaw Ridge is an unmarked, off-piste Black route that runs along beside the cliff edge on the left (looking downhill) of the Saudan Couloir. You can access the top of Chainsaw Ridge by turning left at the top of the 7th Heaven Express Chairlift, going past Horstman Hut, and continuing to the point at the end of the path (do not turn down Blueline). Chainsaw Ridge starts on the left side of this point. You can also access Chainsaw Ridge lower down by taking Upper Green Line (Green), turning onto Panorama (Blue), and then traversing to the right towards the ridge. On a clear day, the views from Chainsaw Ridge are some of the most spectacular in all of Whistler Blackcomb.

> **NOTE**: Accessing and following this route is challenging and should be approached with caution. If it is your first time, ideally go with someone who knows this route. Stay away from the cornice edge, as there is a danger that it might break off, sending you falling down the cliffs along the edge of the couloir.

♦♦♦ False Face: False Face is an extremely steep Triple-Black face that drops into the Saudan Couloir to the left (looking downhill) of the Saudan Couloir run (Double Black). You can access False Face by turning left at the top of the 7th Heaven Express Chairlift, going past Horstman Hut, and skiing to the point at the end of the path. Access to False Face is straight and to the right off the front of the point.

> **NOTE**: This is one of the most challenging skiable faces anywhere in North America. Given the steep slope, there can be very little snow and plenty of exposed rock. This is an expert, freeride skiing zone only.

The view down Chainsaw Ridge towards the top of the Jersey Cream Express Chairlift and Rendezvous Lodge on a fresh snow day. (Source: Dave Brengelmann)

◆◆◆ Hawaii 5-0: Hawaii 5-0 is an extremely steep, curved Triple-Black chute that leads into the Saudan Couloir. The entrance to '5-0' (as the locals call it) is via Chainsaw Ridge (Black), over the cornice, and into the chute below. Hawaii 5-0 gets its name from the 50° angle of the slope in the chute (one of the steepest ski runs in all of North America).

> **NOTE**: Given the steepness of this chute, there can be very little snow and plenty of exposed rock face. Approach only with extreme caution, and make sure there is sufficient snow cover to avoid hitting rocks on the way down.

◆◆ Upper Feather Tree: Upper Feather Tree is a steep, rocky Double-Black slope on the right side (looking downhill) of the Saudan Couloir that leads down into the upper end of couloir. You can access the top of Upper Feathertree via the Sunrise Traverse (Double Black).

> **NOTE**: This is a steep, challenging slope, and it should only be skied when there is sufficient snow to cover the rocks.

♦ **Lower Feather Tree:** Lower Feather Tree is a steep, wide slope on the right side (looking downhill) of the lower part of the Saudan Couloir, above the Jersey Cream Bowl. You can access Lower Feather Tree (Black) via a traverse at the bottom of Upper Feather Tree (Double Black) or from the right side of Quasar (Double Black).

> **NOTE**: When going down this run, be careful to be aware of and avoid the many small trees that could catch your skis and trigger a fall.

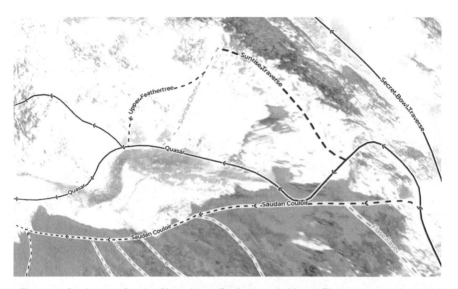

The upper Black runs—Sunrise Chute, Upper Feathertree, and Lower Feathertree—on the south side of the Saudan Couloir. (Source: Openskimap.org)

♦/♦♦ **Lower end of Chainsaw Ridge:** There are a series of Black and Double-Black routes below the lower end of Chainsaw Ridge (Black), near the top of the Jersey Cream Express Chairlift. The most difficult—Regulator (Double Black), Dog Leg (Black), and High Test (Black)—are towards the upper end of this part of the ridge, and the easier ones—Low Test (Black) and Hot Tub (Black)—are at the lower end closer to the top of the Jersey Cream Express Chairlift.

This part of the Saudan Couloir is known for deep snow that accumulates behind the ridge after winter storms.

> **NOTE**: Access to these runs is over the cornice along the edge of Chainsaw Ridge. Approach with caution and make sure you know what is below the cornice before you drop over it.

♦ **Quasar:** Quasar is the easier (but still challenging), steep Black route down into the Saudan Couloir. It starts to the right of the top of the Saudan Couloir (Double Black), goes down the right side (looking downhill) of the couloir, curves to the right side of the moraine that runs down the middle of the couloir, and ends in the top of Jersey Cream Bowl. You can access this run by skiing below Horstman Hut, continuing to the entrance of Blue Line (Blue), and then traversing to the left (looking downhill) to the Quasar entrance.

> **NOTE**: Although this is the easier route into the couloir, it is still a steep and challenging run. The entrance into the couloir at the top of this run is narrow, steep, and often very icy. This is an experts-only run and should be approached with caution.

HISTORY NOTES

Sylvain Saudan

Sylvain Saudan is a famous extreme skier from Switzerland. He is considered to be the father of extreme skiing, which has earned him the name 'skier of the impossible.' To safely ski these mountains, he developed a new technique to 'jump turn' on very steep inclines. He is an accomplished guide for heliskiing and was one of the first European guides to lead tours into the Bugaboos in British Columbia in the 1970s.

Prior to the installation of the 7th Heaven Express Chairlift, local Whistler extreme skiers would hike to the top of Blackcomb Mountain to ski the challenging terrain of the high alpine. They started calling one of the most challenging runs the 'Saudan Couloir' in honor of the father of extreme skiing. The name stuck, and when extreme skiing was exploding in popularity in 1987, Blackcomb launched a race that set off from the top of the Saudan Couloir down into Jersey Cream Bowl.

Sources:

https://www.cbc.ca/news/canada/british-columbia/sylvain-saudan-godfather-of-extreme-skiing-lends-his-name-again-to-blackcomb-mountain-1.4395230

https://en.wikipedia.org/wiki/Sylvain_Saudan

♦♦ **Saudan Couloir:** The Saudan Couloir run is the world-famous, steep Double-Black run down the center of the Saudan Couloir that ends at the top of Jersey Cream Bowl. Access to the Saudan Couloir is via the 7th Heaven Express Chairlift. From there, ski below Horstman Hut, continuing to the entrance of Blue Line (Blue), and then traverse to the left (looking downhill) to the entrance into the couloir.

> **NOTE:** The entrance into the couloir at the top of this run is narrow, steep, and often very icy. This is an experts-only run and should be approached with caution.

Looking up into the Saudan Couloir with the moraine running down the middle.
(Source: Jennifer Nairn)

♦♦ **Sunrise Chute:** Sunrise Chute is a narrow, steep, rocky Double-Black chute accessible at the top from the Sunrise Traverse (Triple Black).

> **NOTE:** This is a very challenging, experts-only chute and should only be skied when there is sufficient snow to cover the rocks.

◆◆ **Sunrise Traverse:** Sunrise Traverse is a narrow, rocky, and challenging Double-Black traverse that goes from the right side (looking downhill) of Quasar (Black) over to the top of a cliff to the top of Sunrise Chute (Double Black).

> **NOTE**: This traverse is very narrow, rocky, and exposed. It should only be approached when there is sufficient snow to cover the rocks.

◆◆◆ **Whiplash:** Similar to Bushrat and Bushwip (both Triple Black), Whiplash is a Triple-Black entrance into the Saudan Couloir below Chainsaw Ridge. The entrance is over a cornice, which then leads into a steep, rocky, chute down into the couloir.

> **NOTE**: The entrance into this run over the cornice is very difficult and can be dangerous depending on conditions.

RESORT INFORMATION

Resort Area

Whistler Blackcomb is a large resort that encompasses several neighborhoods, each with its own unique character and charm. The resort's main hub is Whistler Village, a pedestrian village located at the base of Whistler Mountain. Here, you will find a wide range of accommodations, restaurants, and shops, as well as easy access to ski lifts and gondolas for both Blackcomb and Whistler Mountains. Whistler Village is also home to several lively après-ski venues and entertainment options.

The Olympic Rings in Whistler Village at night. (Source: Nick Jones)

South of Whistler Village is Whistler Creekside. This is the original base area of the resort. Here, visitors will find a more laid-back atmosphere with a variety of accommodations and restaurants catering to families and those seeking a quieter experience.

Whistler Creekside also offers access up onto Whistler Mountain via the Creekside Gondola.

At the base of Blackcomb Mountain are the Blackcomb Upper Village and the Blackcomb Benchlands. These areas offer a combination of upscale hotels and condo rentals. The Blackcomb Upper Village is also home to the Upper Village Market, which features a range of stores and restaurants.

Beyond these main areas, there are other neighborhoods of homes and townhomes as well as golf courses, a rec center, and commercial/industrial areas.

Overall, the layout of the Whistler Blackcomb resort is designed to cater to a wide range of visitors, with something to suit every taste.

Winter Season

The ski season at Whistler Blackcomb typically begins in late November or early December depending on snow conditions and runs until late May (again depending on snow conditions). Towards the end of the season, Whistler Mountain closes first in mid-April, with Blackcomb Mountain continuing to operate until the Victoria Day Weekend, which is around May 21st.

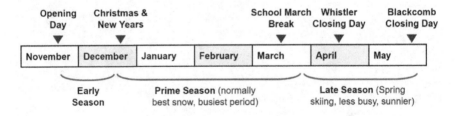

The best snow conditions at Whistler Blackcomb generally occur from mid-December to mid-March, when the resort receives most of its annual snowfall. During this time, temperatures are typically cooler, and storms bring consistent, fresh snow to the slopes. January and February are particularly good months for skiing and snowboarding, with the snowpack reaching its deepest levels and providing optimal conditions for powder skiing. However, it's important to note that weather conditions can vary from year to year—and even within a single season. Visitors should keep an eye on weather reports and snow forecasts to plan their trips accordingly.

As with most ski resorts, the busiest times at Whistler Blackcomb are during the holidays and during the peak season. The Christmas and New Year's holidays, the weeks surrounding the US Presidents' Day and Canadian Family Day, as well as the school March Break period in mid-March tend to be the busiest times, with the resort experiencing high volumes of visitors. The World Ski and Snowboard Festival in April also attracts large crowds. On the other hand, the period between mid-January and mid-February and the months of April and May generally see fewer visitors, making it a great time to enjoy the slopes with fewer crowds.

Spring skiing in April and May can be quite wonderful with warmer weather, long daylight hours and softer snow.

Location

Located just 125 kilometers north of Vancouver, British Columbia, Whistler Blackcomb is easily accessible via the scenic Sea-to-Sky Highway, which winds its way through the picturesque Howe Sound area and breathtaking Coastal Mountain range.

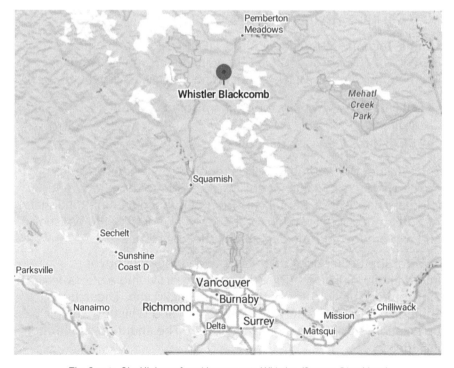

The Sea-to-Sky Highway from Vancouver to Whistler. (Source: Bing Maps)

Transportation

Getting to Whistler Blackcomb is easy, as there are a variety of transportation options available.

The Vancouver International Airport (YVR) is the nearest major airport. YVR is serviced by the major Canadian airlines—Air Canada, WestJet, etc.—as well as many US and international airlines. YVR also has many local/regional airlines—Pacific Coastal Airlines, Central Mountain Air, etc.—that fly into the airport. Outside of the main part of the airport, there is also a seaplane terminal that supports several local seaplane airlines, including Harbour Air and Tofino Air.

- **YVR:** https://www.yvr.ca/en/passengers
- **YVR Airlines:** https://www.yvr.ca/en/passengers/flights/airlines-and-destinations

Another option is the Abbotsford International Airport (YXX), which is about one and a half hours from Vancouver and is serviced by several airlines like WestJet, Swoop, and Flair Airlines.

- **YXX:** https://www.abbotsfordairport.ca/

Seattle-Tacoma International Airport (SEA) is located in the USA about a three-hour drive from Vancouver, and Bellingham International Airport (BLI) is about an hour away across the border.

- **BLI:** https://www.portofbellingham.com/82/Airport-Administration
- **SEA:** https://www.portseattle.org/sea-tac

The Whistler Blackcomb Resort is roughly a two-hour drive from Vancouver by car, making it easily accessible for both local and international visitors. Rental cars from the Vancouver International Airport are a popular option for those who want to get to Whistler and explore the surrounding area at their own pace.

Several shuttle services operate between the Vancouver International Airport (YVR) and the resort, providing a stress-free and comfortable way to reach Whistler Blackcomb. These bus shuttles run regularly between Vancouver and Whistler, with pick-up locations at different points in the city. The shuttle bus operators include:

- **Epic Rides:** https://epicrides.ca/
- **Whistler Shuttle:** https://www.whistlershuttle.com/
- **YVR Skylynx:** https://yvrskylynx.com/

Finally, there are luxury limousine services available that can transport guests from the airport to Whistler in style.

Whistler Village, Creekside, and the Blackcomb Upper Village are all pedestrian-friendly and easy to navigate on foot, with a network of sidewalks and pathways connecting shops, restaurants, and accommodations. For those who prefer not to walk, there is also a bus shuttle service in the resort area that operates throughout the day, stopping at several key locations. Taxis and ride-share services are also available for those looking for another way to get around.

- **Whistler Transit:** https://www.whistler.ca/services/transportation/transit
- **Whistler Resort Cabs:** (604) 938-1515
- **Whistler Taxi:** (604) 932-3333
- **Whistler Taxi Service:** (604) 262-3806

Accommodation

Whistler Village offers a wide variety of accommodation options to suit different budgets and preferences. The resort features several well-known hotel chains, as well as a range of boutique accommodations that offer a more personalized and intimate experience. Some of the properties are ski in/ski out and are located just steps from the ski hills and lifts providing easy access to the slopes. For those looking for a more secluded experience, the surrounding areas offer a range of private rental properties and vacation homes. Additionally, the area is home to a number of rental condominiums and townhomes, which are popular options for families and larger groups.

Whistler Village

Whistler Village is home to the bulk of the accommodations in the resort area. This area includes everything from expensive, high-end hotels to more affordable hotel and condo options as well as the only 'pod hotel' in the resort area. You can also rent private condos or units via online services like Airbnb.

This area is popular with visitors who want easy access to the stores, restaurants, and nightlife in the village as well as pedestrian access to the Whistler and Blackcomb gondolas and lifts situated at the Whistler Village base area. It is worth noting that this area can get quite crowded and noisy, especially during the busy periods of the year.

Upper Village (Blackcomb) and The Blackcomb Benchlands

The Upper Village on Blackcomb offers a more limited range of hotels and condos but is quieter and less crowded than the main village area. It is also a relatively short walk to Whistler Village. The Blackcomb Gondola provides access from this area up onto Blackcomb Mountain.

This area includes two of the high-end hotels in the resort area: the Fairmont Chateau Whistler and the Four Seasons Resort Whistler. These hotels are famous for their quality and style. There are also several other hotels and condo options in this area.

The Blackcomb Benchlands—just uphill from the Blackcomb Upper Village—offers a range of rental options. Some of these are located right next to the hill and offer easy ski-in/ski-out ability: The Aspens, Woodrun, and Blackcomb Suites. Others can be accessed via a short walk to the hill or using the shuttle bus that runs through the area.

Whistler Creekside Village

The Creekside Village area is similar to the Blackcomb Upper Village in that it tends to be quieter and not as busy as the main village. This area includes several hotel/condo-style accommodations—Nitka Lake Lodge, Legends, Lake Placid Lodge, First Tracks Lodge, etc.—as well as many other private condo, townhouse, or home-rental options.

Creekside Village offers visitors quick access to the mountain via the Creekside Gondola and includes a limited number of stores and restaurants.

Other Options

Beyond the three village areas, there are a wide range of rental accommodation options available in the resort area, including apartments, condos, townhouses, and homes/chalets. These areas are quieter and more private, but you will need to drive or take a bus to get to the hill to ski.

The best way to find accommodation in the resort area is to use sites such as:

- **Airbnb:** https://www.airbnb.ca/
- **Alluradirect:** https://www.alluradirect.com/
- **Booking.com:** https://www.booking.com/
- **Expedia:** https://www.expedia.com/
- **VRBO:** https://www.vrbo.com/
- **Whistler.com:** https://www.whistler.com/accommodation
- **Whistler Blackcomb:** https://www.whistlerblackcomb.com/plan-your-trip/stay/whistler-blackcomb-lodging.aspx

Restaurants and Bars

There are a wide range of restaurants and bars in the Whistler Blackcomb Resort area. Whistler Tourism keeps a good, updated list of restaurants and bars at https://www.whistler.com/dining/.

For casual après-ski drinks and food, Dusty's Bar and BBQ in Creekside, Merlin's Bar and Grill in the Upper Village, and the Garibaldi Lift Co. Bar and Grill at the Whistler Village base are good options to consider. There is also the Dubh Linn Gate Irish Pub for Irish pub fare and Longhorn Saloon for a hopping après-ski party experience.

If you are looking for breakfast, lunch, or dinner, there are numerous options available throughout the resort area including cafes, bakeries, pizza, Italian food, Indian food, Mexican food, tapas, sushi, pub food, steak houses, and high-end restaurants.

Stores

The Whistler Blackcomb Resort offers a range of shopping options. Visitors can find everything from high-end boutiques to outdoor gear stores to souvenir shops to food and liquor stores. Whistler Village is home to several luxury fashion brands, such as Prada and Gucci, as well as high-end outdoor retailers like Arc'teryx, Patagonia, and The North Face. For those looking for more affordable options, there are also several retail chains and independent stores offering ski gear, clothing, accessories, and gifts. Additionally, there are specialty stores focusing on locally made products, such as pottery, jewelry, and artwork.

Grocery Stores

There are several grocery stores to meet the needs of both visitors and locals in the Whistler area. The larger supermarkets include Nesters Market, IGA grocery store, and the Fresh St. Market. The Fresh St. Market is the largest and offers a wide range of fresh produce, meats, dairy products, and staples. In addition to the larger grocery stores, there are also several smaller markets and specialty stores selling groceries, organic and gourmet products, as well as health food and supplements.

If you are driving through Squamish on your way up to Whistler, consider stopping and picking up groceries there, as it will be cheaper than what you will find in Whistler. The Save-On-Foods in Squamish is a good option, as is the Nesters Market if you are looking for more upscale gourmet foods.

Liquor Stores

The Whistler area has several liquor stores to cater to the needs of its visitors and residents. The British Columbia Liquor Distribution Branch (BCLDB) operates three government-run liquor stores in Whistler, offering a wide selection of beer, wine, and spirits. In addition to the BCLDB stores, there are also several privately owned wine and spirits shops in Whistler, including the Whistler Beer and Wine Store, Blackcomb Liquor Store, and Summit Lodge Boutique Hotel Liquor Store. These stores offer a selection of premium wines, craft beers, and unique spirits, as well as knowledgeable staff who can offer advice on pairings and make recommendations.

Ski and Board Shops

Whistler is home to several large ski and board shops, including Can-Ski, Evo, Spicy Sports, and Summit Sport. Most of these stores also offer equipment rentals as well as tuning and repair services. In addition, there are several specialty stores selling high-end ski and snowboarding gear, such as The North Face, Salomon, Peak Performance and Burton. The stores in the resort area offer a range of clothing, accessories, and equipment for all levels of skiers and snowboarders, from beginners to experts. They also have knowledgeable staff who can offer advice on gear selection and fitting.

Tuning and Repair Shops

Beyond ski shops that also offer tuning and repair services, there are a couple of dedicated shops in the resort area that focus on these services, including: Alpine Pro Ski and Boot Services Whistler (Blackcomb Base), Profile Ski and Snowboard Services, and Underground Tuning (Whistler Village).

Health Care

In Whistler Village, the Whistler Health Care Centre, located at 4380 Lorimer Road, is a well-equipped facility providing urgent care, X-ray, and laboratory services to address immediate medical needs. Additionally, the resort includes several walk-in clinics, pharmacies, and private practices to cater to a variety of health-care needs.

- **Whistler Health Care Center:** https://www.vch.ca/en/location/whistler-health-care-centre
- **Whistler Medical Clinic:** http://whistlermedicalclinic.com/

For more advanced care or emergencies, the nearest full-service hospital is Squamish General Hospital, situated approximately 60 kilometers south of Whistler at 38140 Behrner Drive, Squamish. This hospital offers a 24-hour emergency room, inpatient care, diagnostic services, and a range of specialized medical services.

- **Squamish General Hospital:** https://www.vch.ca/en/location/squamish-general-hospital

Whistler Blackcomb is a hub for events and festivals that take place during the ski season. One of the most anticipated events each year is the World Ski and Snowboard Festival, which takes place in April and includes a range of competitions, concerts, and art exhibits. In January, the Whistler Film Festival attracts film enthusiasts from all over the world, featuring a lineup of independent and international films as well as industry workshops and panels. Additionally, Whistler Blackcomb hosts a range of holiday-themed events throughout the winter season, including Christmas markets, New Year's Eve parties, and a variety of family-friendly activities.

Here are some specific events that take place during the ski season at Whistler Blackcomb:

- **Whistler Holiday Market (December):** The Whistler Holiday Market includes two days of local art, holiday spirit, and artisanal treats.
  https://artswhistler.com/holiday-market:
- **Fire and Ice Show (Sundays, December to March):** The Fire and Ice Show is a free event for visitors on Sunday evenings all winter with athletic feats, music, cultural sharing, and fireworks.
  https://www.whistlerblackcomb.com/explore-the-resort/activities-and-events/winter-activities/fire-and-ice.aspx:
- **Whistler Pride and Ski Festival (January):** The Pride and Ski Festival is a week packed with winter sport, culture, and entertainment. https://whistlerpride.com/
- **Whistler Film Festival (January):** The WFF includes film premieres, industry summits, talent programs, parties, and special guest appearances by actors and directors.
  https://whistlerfilmfestival.com/
- **Peak to Creek Race (February):** The Peak to Creek Race is the longest GS race of its kind on the planet, challenging teams of four to race down Whistler Mountain.
  https://www.whistler.com/blog/post/2023/01/11/whistler-peak-to-valley-race

- **World Ski and Snowboard Festival (April):** The WSSF is an annual spring celebration of snow sports, music, arts, and mountain culture.
  https://wssf.com/

Whistler also hosts a range of ski-racing events and off-piste freeride events throughout the winter season.

Please note that the events schedule may vary from year to year, so it's always a good idea to check the local Whistler websites for the most up-to-date information.

- **Whistler Blackcomb Events:** https://www.whistlerblackcomb.com/explore-the-resort/activities-and-events/events.aspx
- **Whistler Tourism Events:** https://www.whistler.com/events/

While skiing and snowboarding are the main attractions in Whistler during winter, there are also plenty of other activities to enjoy. One popular option is snowshoeing, which allows visitors to explore the stunning winter landscape and enjoy the snow-covered forests and mountains at a more leisurely pace. Visitors can also take part in dog sledding, where they can ride on a sled pulled by a team of Huskies and experience the thrill of gliding through the snow. For those who want a faster pace, there are several options for snowmobiling around the resort area. If you want to relax and rejuvenate, there are several spas in Whistler offering massages, facials, and hot-stone therapy. Additionally, visitors can take a scenic helicopter tour of the area to enjoy the breathtaking views of the surrounding mountains and glaciers.

Outdoor Adventures/Activities

- **Brandywine Falls Park:** Brandywine Falls Park offers a beautiful walk/snowshoe to a stunning waterfall.
https://bcparks.ca/brandywine-falls-park/
- **Crystal Hut Fondue:** Skidoo up to the Crystal Hut for a dinner fondue!
https://www.canadianwilderness.com/whistler/fondue-dinner/
- **Dog Sledding:** There are several dog sledding options in Whistler that let you live out your Iditarod dreams!
https://www.whistler.com/activities/dog-sledding/
- **Lost Lake Park:** Lost Lake Park offers snowshoeing and cross-country skiing and has a rental shop if you don't have your own gear.
https://www.whistler.com/activities/nordic-skiing/lost-lake-park/
- **Scandinave Spa:** Scandinave offers a wonderful outdoor spa but has a no-talking rule.
https://temp.scandinave.com/whistler/
- **Snowmobiling:** There are several snowmobiling options in the area to service everything from families to those looking for backcountry adventures.
https://www.whistler.com/activities/snowmobiling/#one

- **Superfly Ziplines:** Superfly lives up to its name, letting you zip along up to 100 kilometers per hour, 200 meters above the ground!
  https://superflyziplines.com/ziplines/
- **Whistler Tube Park:** The Whistler Tube Park offers a range of sliding options from easier to more expert down a 1000-foot-long run!
  https://www.whistler.com/activities/tube-park

Kids getting ready to go down the Tube Park!
(Source: Caroline Pocock)

- **Vallea Lumina:** Vallea Lumina offers a magical night-time walk through a forest of lights.
  https://vallealumina.com/
- **Valley Trail:** The Valley Trail offers a range of walking options through the valley.
  https://www.whistler.com/activities/valley-trail
- **Village Walk:** The Village Walk is a great stroll through Whistler Village where you can check out the shops, galleries, restaurants, and coffee shops.
  https://cdn.whistler.com/s3/pdf/maps/whistler-map-2021-large.pdf

- **Whistler Olympic Park (Callaghan Valley):** The Whistler Olympic Park offers both snowshoeing and cross-country skiing along with a rental shop if you don't have your own gear. https://www.whistler.com/activities/nordic-skiing/whistler-olympic-park/
- **Whistler Sliding Center:** The Whistler Sliding Center lets you live your Olympic dream of shooting down the track in a Bobsleigh! https://www.whistlersportlegacies.com/whistler-sliding-centre/overview
- **Ziptrek Zipline:** Ziptrek offers the longest zipline in Canada! https://whistler.ziptrek.com/

Indoor Activities

- **Art Galleries:** There are several art galleries in the resort area. https://www.whistler.com/arts/#galleries
- **Audain Art Museum:** The Audain Art Museum is the large black spaceship building next to the parking lots in the Whistler Village area. https://www.whistler.com/arts/audain-art-museum/
- **Escape Whistler:** Escape Whistler offers themed challenges where players collaborate to find clues, complete tasks, and solve a variety of puzzles. https://escapewhistler.com/
- **Meadows Park Rec Center:** The Rec Center offers pools, hot tubs, squash courts, a fitness center, and an ice rink. https://www.whistler.ca/culture-recreation/facilities/meadow-park-sports-centre
- **Spas:** There are several spas in the resort area for your relaxation needs. https://www.whistler.com/wellness
- **Squamish Lil'wat Cultural Centre:** The Cultural Center is a great way to find out more about the First Nations culture and history of the area. https://www.whistler.com/arts/squamish-lilwat-cultural-centre/
- **Vodka Ice Room (Bearfoot Bistro):** Visit the Vodka Ice Room where you get to wear a parka as you try high-end vodka. https://www.exploretock.com/keteloneiceroom/

- **Whistler Distillery Tour and Tasting Experience:** Visit the Whistler Distillery to taste fine, locally made alcohols. https://www.whistler.com/blog/post/2021/08/17/whistler-distillery-tour/
- **Whistler Museum:** Find out about the history of the Whistler Blackcomb area at the Whistler Museum. https://www.whistler.com/arts/museum/

SKIING TERMINOLOGY

*I*f you have not already heard them where you ski, you might hear some new terms on Whistler Blackcomb, including the ones below. There are also many fun combinations of these terms, for example: Shred the gnar (pronounced 'shred the nar') meaning 'to ski fast and aggressively with skill and style through challenging or difficult ski runs or terrain park features.'

7th: 7th is the short form for the 7th Heaven Express Chairlift area.

Alpine Zone: The alpine zone is the high-elevation zone of the mountain where trees do not grow and snow conditions can be harsher (and/or amazing, depending on the day).

AST: AST stands for Avalanche Safety Training. Skiers and boarders who go into the backcountry should take AST courses so that they can avoid avalanches and deal with them if they happen.

Avalanche: An avalanche is a large mass of snow that breaks off from the side of a mountain and slides downhill at a very high speed. A 'full slab' avalanche is the most dangerous type of avalanche and occurs when a whole side of a slope or hill breaks off as a single slab and slides downhill. Avalanches can be very dangerous and can break away trees, wreck buildings, and bury skiers and snowboarders.

Backcountry: The backcountry is the area of unmarked and unpatrolled terrain outside of a ski resort's boundaries.

Backside: The backside is the part of the mountain opposite the resort, usually on the 'back side' of the mountain.

Base: The base is the area of the resort at the bottom of the mountain where lifts, ticket offices, and other facilities are located. It is also used to describe the area at the bottom of a chairlift or gondola.

Bluebird: A bluebird is a day with clear, blue, sunny skies. Some people also use it to specifically describe a day with fresh powder snow and clear, sunny skies.

Boot Hike: A boot hike is an uphill path where you need to take off your skis, carry them, and hike up to get access to another part of the mountain.

Bowl: A bowl is a wide, open area on the mountain with surrounding terrain that often allows for big turns and high-speed skiing. Bowls are formed by glaciers over time when the glacial ice cracks and grinds away the underlying rock.

Bumps: Bumps is another name for moguls or other bumpy terrain on a run.

Chair: Chair is the short-form name for chairlift.

Chairlift: A chairlift is a cable system used at ski resorts to carry skiers and snowboarders up the slopes. It includes a series of seats or chairs attached to overhead cables that allow passengers to sit as they are carried uphill. Chairlifts normally have a safety barrier that is pulled down and a lower bar on which to rest your skis.

Chatter: Chatter is the noise that occurs when you are skiing at high speed over hard snow and your ski begins to vibrate.

Chonky: Chonky is another way of saying big, fat, or large. For example, 'Those were some chonky bumps!'

Closed Area: A closed area is an area on the mountain that the ski patrol has determined to be dangerous and should not be skied. People who ski into a closed area risk losing their ski pass if they are caught by the ski patrol.

Cold Front: A cold front is a weather-related term that describes the leading edge of an oncoming mass of cold air. Cold fronts can trigger snow and can also result in a rapid drop in temperature.

Corduroy: Corduroy is another name for the grooved surface of a freshly groomed run. Sometimes it is shortened to just 'cordo'.

Corn Snow: Corn snow occurs when the snow melts and freezes, forming large granules (about the size of a kernel of corn) that often end up in mounds on the runs. Corn snow typically occurs in spring as temperatures rise.

Cornice: A cornice is an overhanging ledge of snow and ice that forms along the edge of a ridge. They are created as wind blows over the ridge and deposits snow on the downwind side.

Couloir: A couloir is a steep valley or gully on the side of a mountain.

Crispy: There are two uses for this word related to skiing. You can say it is a crispy day when the air is cold and crisp. You can also use crispy to describe a freshly groomed run that is cold and great for carving. For example, "That was a sweet crispy run that we just ripped down!"

Crud: Crud is snow that has been broken up into chunks or clumps by previous skiers, making it difficult to ski through. A worse version of crud is 'ice crud', where chunky, clumpy snow has melted and then frozen.

Crust: A crust occurs when rain falls on top of new snow or the upper layer of snow melts due to warm temperatures followed by freezing temperatures. This can result in challenging skiing conditions as your skis break through and get stuck under the crust.

Download: To download is when you take a lift or gondola down to a base area instead of skiing out to the base at the end of the day.

Drop/Dropping: To drop is when someone jumps off a cliff or lip into the area below. By calling out "dropping!" before you drop, you are warning others that you are about to drop down.

Dust on Crust: Dust on crust is when there is only a 'dusting' of new snow covering harder, icy snow underneath.

Excalibur: Excalibur is the short-form name for the Excalibur Gondola.

Excelerator: Excelerator is the short-form name for the Excelerator Express Chairlift.

Exposure: Exposure refers to the level of risk or danger associated with skiing a particular area or run as a result of steepness, potential for avalanches, cliffs, rock fall, crevasses, etc. Many of the Double and Triple-Black runs in the resort have high exposure as they are steep, narrow, and surrounded by rocks and cliffs.

Face: A face is a very steep section of a mountain. It is a prominent and relatively unbroken surface, usually characterized by its incline and the challenges it presents to skiers and snowboarders. One of the famous faces in the resort is the False Face at the top of the Saudan Couloir on Blackcomb.

Face Shot: A face shot occurs when someone is skiing or snowboarding in deep powder and they get a face full of snow because of a jump or turn.

Fluffy Bumps: Fluffy bumps are moguls or other bumps covered in fresh powder snow! One of the great joys of skiing at Whistler Blackcomb is finding untouched fluffy bumps on a fresh powder day!

Freeride: Freeride refers to snowboarding or skiing on natural, ungroomed terrain, without a set course, goals, or rules. Freeriding also often suggests a level of difficulty and expertise above normal resort skiing.

Freestyle: Freestyle is when skiers and snowboarders perform aerial flips and spins, box and rail slides, and other tricks. This is normally done in a terrain park area but can also happen anywhere on the mountain.

French Fries: French fries is a fun term ski instructors use to describe how to ski with your skies in a parallel stance (side by side like French Fries).

Frontside: The frontside is the part of the mountain facing the resort, typically groomed and with easier terrain.

Freshies: Finding or skiing 'freshies' is when you are able to ski on fresh/new snow.

Frosty: Frosty is a term to describe a very cold day and/or cold temperatures.

Glacier: A glacier is a large mass of ice that forms over many years as snow accumulates and compacts into ice. Glaciers usually form on the north-facing sides of mountains that are in the shade and as a result experience less melting than the south-facing side of the mountain.

Glades: Glades are ungroomed runs or areas of the mountain with trees. The spacing between the trees, the steepness of the run, and other factors result in varying glade difficulty levels.

Gnarly: Gnarly (the 'g' is silent) is used to describe a challenging or difficult ski run or terrain park feature. Gnarly originally comes from surfing culture, where it was used to describe challenging, difficult wave conditions.

Gondola: A gondola is an enclosed cabin system designed to transport skiers, snowboarders, and sightseers up and down a mountain. Gondolas are suspended from a continuously moving cable and carry eight to twelve (or more) passengers and their equipment. Skis and boards are often stored on racks on the outside of the gondola.

Gondy: Gondy is a fun short-form name for gondolas.

Groomers: This word has three meanings. Groomers are the large, tracked machines that are used to flatten and smooth runs at a ski resort. Groomers are also the staff that operate these machines. And finally, groomers is also used to describe the runs that have been groomed.

Halfpipe: A halfpipe is a large U-shaped feature in the terrain park used for skiing or snowboarding tricks and jumps.

Hardpack: Hardpack is snow that has been compressed and hardened by skiers and snowboarders. It creates a smooth and fast surface but can also be slippery/icy and difficult to control.

Hut: A hut is a smaller building on the mountain that normally offers limited food/snacks, a place to warm up, and washrooms.

Ice: Ice on a ski hill is usually formed when snow has frozen and hardened, making it challenging and potentially dangerous to ski on. Ice can also form on runs as a result of heavy traffic down the run that turns the snow to ice.

Ice Bombs: Ice bombs are chunks of frozen, icy snow stuck to the surface of a run. They look soft, but when you hit them, it feels like hitting a rock! The ice bombs on 7th Heaven are legendary!

Jersey Cream: Jersey Cream or just Jersey are short-form names for the Jersey Cream Express Chairlift and the area serviced by that lift.

Jib/Jibbing: To jib or jibbing is to ride on top of rails, boxes, or other obstacles in a terrain park.

Lap: A lap is one complete run around a defined circuit. When skiing, you do laps down a run or a combination of runs, taking a gondola or chairlift to get back to the top of the run again. For example, people who want to achieve a high vertical day will do laps in the Garbanzo Express Chairlift area.

Lodge: A lodge is a larger building on the mountain that offers a range of food and drink options, may have a sit-down restaurant, offers washrooms, may have a gear shop, often has one or more decks, and offers extensive indoor seating.

Moguls: Moguls are bumps that form on the mountain from skiers repeatedly turning and carving on the snow.

Off-Piste: Off-piste is the area that is outside of the marked runs or pistes on a mountain. Off-piste skiing typically includes bumps, trees, ungroomed snow, powder snow, etc.

Open Alpine: The open alpine is the area on a mountain above the tree line where there are no trees. On a fresh powder day, the open alpine is the go-to zone for large areas of untracked powder skiing.

Out of Bounds: Out of bounds refers to the areas on the hill that are outside of the ski resort boundaries. These areas are not patrolled and should not be entered unless you are fully prepared for out-of-bounds or backcountry skiing.

Packed Powder: Packed powder is snow that has been compacted by grooming machines, creating a smooth surface that is easy to ski on. It is often found on groomed runs and is popular with beginners.

Park Rats: Park Rats is a fun term for the young skiers and snowboarders who spend their time skiing in the terrain park areas. Park Rats often wear a distinctive style of baggy clothing that makes them stand out from others on the hill.

Peak: The Peak is the short-form name for Whistler Peak. The Peak Express Chairlift is often just called Peak Chair.

Pineapple Express: A pineapple express is a weather system that is characterized by a stream of warm, moist air originating from the Pacific Ocean. The name comes from the fact that these systems often originate near Hawaii, which is known for its pineapple plantations.

Piste: Piste is the European term for a ski run (in French it means path or trail). A piste is a marked ski run or path down a mountain for skiing or snowboarding.

Pizza: Pizza is a fun term used by ski instructors to describe to students the stance of skiing with your skis in a V pattern. Skiing with your skis in a V pattern is a good way for beginners to learn how to control their speed.

Pow: Pow is a short-form name for powder snow. As with many skiing terms, it can be creatively combined: "Woo hoo...that was some sweet, crispy pow pow!"

Powder Snow: Powder snow is fresh, light, dry snow that is wonderful for skiing and snowboarding. Skiing in powder is quite different from skiing on groomers and takes some practice to get used to as you are skiing/floating through the snow versus just skiing on top of it.

Proline Runs: Proline runs are the most difficult runs on the mountain. They are also sometimes referred to as Triple-Black runs.

Ridge: A ridge is a narrow, long, elevated area on the mountain that often separates different runs or sections of the mountain. Harmony Ridge on Whistler, for example, is the ridge that runs between Harmony and Symphony Bowls.

Ripper: Ripper is a fun name for a skilled skier or snowboarder. Young kids who are aggressively skiing down the mountain are called young rippers.

Run: A run is a marked ski route or path down a mountain for skiing or snowboarding. The terms run and piste mean the same thing.

Sastrugi: Sastrugi is the name for snow that has been blown into dense ridges by strong winds. The word originates from Russia.

Schuss: A schuss is a straight downhill run with no turns or stops, often used to gain speed. Schuss means 'shot' in German.

Scratchy: Scratchy is used to describe hard/icy terrain that makes a scratching sound as skiers or boarders go down them.

Send It: To send it is to commit to a jump or trick with confidence and determination. Young rippers will often encourage their fellow skiers or boarders to 'send it'. A sender is a skier or boarder who regularly 'sends it'.

Shred: To shred is to ski fast and aggressively with skill and style. A shredder is someone who skies fast and aggressively with skill and style.

Side-country: The side-country is terrain outside of the ski resort's boundaries, but easily accessible from the resort.

Skiing Out: Skiing out is when you ski down to the base of the mountain at the end of the day. If you don't want to ski out, you can always download on a lift or gondola.

Slay/Slay It: To slay something or to slay it is to do something with style and skill. For example, "He slayed that jump!"

Slope: A slope is an inclined surface of a mountain or hill on which skiing and boarding takes place. Slopes can vary in steepness, length, and difficulty, catering to different skill levels.

Sluff: A sluff is a type of avalanche that occurs when a small amount of fresh snow slides off a slope. Sluffs are less dangerous than full slab avalanches.

Slush: Slush is wet, heavy snow that is partially melted (it often includes water) and can be difficult to ski through. It is often found on warmer days or in the spring when the snow begins to melt.

Snorkeling: Snorkeling occurs when you are skiing in very deep powder snow (pow) that almost fully covers your entire body. It is so deep that it is like going snorkeling in the ocean.

Snowplow: A snowplow is a basic ski maneuver used by instructors for beginners. It is similar to the 'pizza', where the skis are pointed inward in a V shape to slow down and control speed.

Soft-pack: Soft-pack snow surface occurs when freshly fallen snow has been somewhat compressed by groomers and skiers. This type of snow offers great skiing, as it provides a good grip for skis and boards.

Snow Snakes: Snow snakes is a fun term used to describe to kids the hard-to-see bumps, small trees, or other surface features that can cause a beginner to wobble and/or fall. "Watch out that the snow snakes don't get you!"

Spicey: Things are spicey when there is challenging weather or snow and/or when you are attempting to do something difficult. "That was some spicey weather today!"

Stomp It: To stomp it is to land a trick or jump solidly and smoothly with style. "He really stomped it!"

Summit: The summit is the highest point of the mountain. Whistler Peak is the summit of Whistler Mountain.

Sundog: Sundogs are the bright spots that appear parallel to the horizon along the outer edge of sun halos.

Sun Halo: A sun halo is caused by the refraction, reflection, and dispersion of light through ice particles suspended within thin, wispy, high-altitude clouds. Light bends at an angle as it passes through these ice crystals, creating a circular halo around the sun.

Terrain Park: A terrain park is a designated area of the mountain with features such as rails, boxes, jumps, and other obstacles for freestyle skiing and snowboarding. Terrain parks come in all sizes, including those for beginners, intermediate, and expert skiers and boarders.

Thigh Burner: A thigh burner is a long run skied without stopping, causing pain in the legs. For example, Peak to Creek on Whistler—11 kilometers from top to bottom—is a real thigh burner!

Tree Line: The tree line is the elevation on the mountain above which trees do not grow. Above the tree line you will find the open alpine zone.

Ungroomed Snow: Ungroomed snow is snow that has not been touched by grooming machines or skiers, creating a more natural and challenging skiing experience. It can be uneven and unpredictable, with varying depths and textures.

Warm Front: A warm front is an approaching edge of a warm, wet mass of air. Snow often falls when a warm front collides with a cold air mass. Whistler Blackcomb often gets warm fronts coming in from the Pacific that result in the wonderful snow that the resort enjoys.

Wet Snow: Wet snow occurs when temperatures are quite warm. As a result, the snow feels wet as it falls and melts easily.

Wind Slab: A wing slab is a layer of relatively stiff, hard snow formed by deposits of windblown snow on the side of a ridge or other sheltered area. Wind slabs can form over weaker, softer freshly fallen powder snow, creating an avalanche hazard on steep slopes.

Windblown Snow: Windblown snow occurs when snow has been blown around by strong winds, creating variable and challenging conditions. It can create drifts and exposed areas of icy or hard-packed snow.

Wishbone: Wishbone is the term used to describe the process of walking up a slope with your skis at an angle on each side (to prevent you from sliding back down the hill). The resulting pattern in the snow looks like the shape of a chicken's wishbone.

Yard Sale: A yard sale is a humorous term to describe when someone crashes and their skis, poles, etc. are scattered across the hillside.

THANKS AND HAVE FUN SKIING!

*T*hank you for choosing this guidebook as a source of information about your visit to Whistler Blackcomb! I hope you enjoyed reading about this world-renowned ski resort and the great skiing it has to offer. I wrote this guidebook with the aim of helping new and existing visitors to Whistler Blackcomb to better understand the resort area, the gondolas/chairs, and the runs on these two mountains.

I wish you a safe and enjoyable visit to Whistler Blackcomb, and I hope this guidebook helps you make unforgettable memories during your visit to this beautiful mountain paradise.

Nick Jones
West Vancouver, BC, Canada

That's me at the top of 7th Heaven with Whistler in the background.
(Source: Nick Jones)

Made in the USA
Las Vegas, NV
09 March 2024

86934902R10154